60 MOST MEMORABLE SALES

From Selling Power *Readers*

60 MOST
MEMORABLE
SALES

From Selling Power Readers

60 Most Memorable Sales from Selling Power Readers
Copyright ©2003 by Personal Selling Power Inc.
All rights reserved. Printed in the U.S.A.
No part of this book may be reproduced or
copied in any form without written
permission from the publisher.

60 Most Memorable Sales from Selling Power Readers
is published in the United States
by Personal Selling Power Inc.
PO Box 5467, Fredericksburg, VA 22403-0467
Phone 540/752-7000

www.sellingpower.com

Cover and book designed by Tarver Harris. Illustrations by Tim Robinson.
Library of Congress Control Number: 2003098352

ISBN # 0-939613-40-9

ACKNOWLEDGMENTS

First and foremost I would like to thank the *Selling Power* readers past and present who have shared the stories of their most memorable sales. The lessons they learned in their interactions with prospects and customers inspired this book. Many sales training and motivational experts also have contributed their sound selling advice to this book and we thank them for their generosity both with ideas and experiences and with their time and effort. (A directory of the contributing experts is included at the back of the book.) For editing these ideas as supplements to the memorable sales we thank Dana Ray and Jacklyn Boice, the editors of this book. Thanks also to Tarver Harris, who designed the book for visual appeal and readability, and art director Colleen McCudden, who supervised the book layout. Proofreader Sally Dunning meticulously checked the final copy for syntax, spelling errors and typos. With his usual attention to detail, production manager Jeff Macharyas oversaw the printing and binding. To the entire team at *Selling Power* I want to express my ongoing thanks for their commitment to quality products and content.

Gerhard Gschwandtner
Publisher

TABLE OF CONTENTS

#1 Be Prepared   I

#2 Creative Closings   3

#3 Ask and You Shall Receive   4

#4 Getting Past Gatekeepers   6

#5 My Sales Gamble   8

#6 Know Your Competition   10

#7 Limitless Opportunities   11

#8 Selling with a Personal Touch   12

#9 Giving All You've Got   14

#10 Competitive Bidding   15

#11 Give Up? Never!   17

#12 Don't Take No for an Answer   19

#13 Providing Customer Service   20

#14 Accentuate the Positive Points   22

#15 Closing with Flair   23

#16 Writing Better Sales Letters   24

#17 Winning Back Lost Customers   26

#18 Creating the Right Presentation   27

#19 Improving Listening Skills   28

#20 Add Variety to Your Selling   30

#21 Cold Calls Yield Results   32

#22 Follow the Customer's Lead   34

#23 Sell Quality, Not Price   35

#24 What Your Customer Needs   36

#25 Persistence Pays Off   38

#26 Don't Be Caught Unprepared   39

#27 Getting Your Foot in the Door   40

#28 Show What You Know   42

#29 Effective Qualifying   43

#30 Customer Appreciation   45

#31 Networking Skills   46

#32 Food for Thought   48

#33 Visualizing Yields Results   49

#34 Establishing Rapport   50

#35 The Power of Prayer   51

#36 Overcoming Objections   52

#37 Adding Value   54

#38 Gatekeeper as Customer   55

#39 Former Customers Aren't "Lost"   57

#40 Going Above and Beyond   58

#41 Tailor Solutions   59

#42 The Little Company Wins Big   61

#43 The Importance of Integrity   62

#44 Make an Impression   64

#45 Follow Universal Teachings   66

#46 Better Brainstorming   67

#47 Expect the Unexpected   68

#48 Unforgettable Final Offers   70

#49 The Power of Concentration   71

#50 Honesty Is the Best Policy   73

#51 Customers Are Number One   74

#52 Double the Sales   77

#53 The Oooh-Aaah Close   78

#54 A Tie to the Rescue   79

#55 Upselling Techniques   80

#56 Keeping Nerves under Control   82

#57 Follow-Up Is International   83

#58 Out of This World   85

#59 Using a Low-Key Approach   86

#60 Asking for Referrals   87

Contributing Experts Directory   91

Index   97

Sale #1

Be Prepared

WHEN OPPORTUNITY KNOCKS...BE PREPARED

After three months of struggling in my new photo business, I had made some progress producing slides for Sears Roebuck and Company. My company had produced some slides for a Mr. Telling's secretary, and she seemed very pleased. After first seeing the slides, she made a few changes and I was to deliver them to her the following Thursday.

In those days, on Thursdays I practiced with a juggling troupe. On that particular Thursday I was dressed in my usual very casual style – a T-shirt with an illustration of skydivers and the slogan *Eat (expletive deleted), Skydive!* Although it sounds crude in print, the T-shirt was tastefully done. You had to look very close to read the slogan. I was wearing sandals and had my hair pulled back into a ponytail. I carried my juggling equipment in a large camera bag.

I stopped off on the way to practice to drop off Mr. Telling's slides. As I stepped off the elevator, his secretary said, "Stuart, Mr. Telling wants to see you right now!" She showed me to his office about 30 floors higher up in the building. I walked in and there sat the top three officers of Sears Roebuck and Company! Mr. Telling, in his gravelly voice, said, "Young man, I have a project I might want you to do, but first tell me about your company and what you do that makes you think I should hand this program over to you, especially dressed the way you are. You have five minutes."

I had two choices. I could impress these men or jump out the window! Since I didn't have a parachute, I decided on making an impression. I picked out three colored lacrosse balls from my juggling bag and started my presentation.

"Light Productions is a company based on three basic truths. First, the customer deserves great service; second, the customer deserves a good price; third, the customer should be entertained at all times," I rattled off. Then I tossed the balls into the air, twirled around and started juggling. Dead silence.

When I had finished, I bowed and said, "Mr. Telling, I would be honored if you trusted me with your program. How soon can we get started?" Mr. Telling replied, "Quite an act, son. I hope your slides are as good. See my secretary about the details. Oh, and get a haircut." Then they all laughed.

That account turned out to be worth $300,000 a year and it taught me a valuable lesson – always look professional because you never know when opportunity might knock on your door.

– Submitted by Stuart N. Van Dorn

Catch your prospect's eye

You don't have to juggle or turn backflips to keep customers visually engaged - just spice up bland charts and graphs with supporting visuals that reinforce your ideas. Chambers & Asher Speechworks co-founder Spring Asher offers the following ideas for memorable visuals that highlight your product and make you stand out.

1. Use drawings of grocery bags to compare highs and lows in food sales over a multiyear period.

2. Put a large building next to a smaller one to show which construction company has more sales.

3. Chart the ups and downs of a cruise line's operations as the course of a ship's cruise.

4. Choose a pizza, wheel, clock, coin or a cross-cut of a tree log to **make an effective pie chart**.

5. Picture a dollar bill being passed from hand to hand to **represent the term** *cash flow*.

6. Draw an exit sign to reinforce the word *downsizing* in a presentation.

7. Use a photograph of a forest as the background visual for a presentation on the environment.

Asher cites *USA Today* as a source of great ideas for stimulating visuals. "If you think about the trends in communications today, your visuals are really about storytelling - helping you connect with your customers."

Spring Asher
Chambers &
Asher Speechworks

Sale #2
Creative Closings
RRRRIP...I WATCHED MY PROSPECT'S JAW DROP

At the beginning of my sales career I stumbled across a tape series by J. Douglas Edwards that gave me many ideas. During my first year in the field, having listened to his tape series, I made a conscious effort to try something from it every day.

Every Thursday morning, like clockwork, I visited with the top decision maker of one of our major accounts. On every call I presented new ideas. After about six months of pounding my head against the wall without getting any further I asked myself, "What can I do differently?" The idea came to me out of the blue, thanks to J. Douglas Edwards. I hurried down to my bank, went up to one of the tellers and withdrew $100 from my account in the form of a single $100 bill. Before leaving the bank I asked, "If I rip this bill up but keep the pieces can I return it for its full value?" The teller looked puzzled but assured me that if the serial code matched there would not be a problem.

I couldn't wait until Thursday morning. On the way to the account I popped the tape in the car and visualized the closing technique I was about to use. The buyer greeted me in his normal friendly fashion and I asked him if he had recently purchased anything from our competition. He smiled and said yes, and with that I took out the $100 bill and asked a simple question: "Do you know what this is?"

He took it and said, "Looks like the real McCoy to me." I then took the bill back, said, "This is what you are doing with your money" and ripped up the bill. His jaw dropped. "Are you crazy?" he yelled. I smiled and replied, "No more than you are for not taking advantage of Cost Containment." We spoke for a while about our program and I thanked him for his time and headed on to make other calls.

By the time I got back to my office there was a call from my prospect asking me to come back to the facility the next day to meet with his boss. I arrived early the next day, gave an overview of our capabilities and Cost Containment and walked out with a three-year commitment. It just goes to show that creativity can make the difference.

By the way, I did take the ripped $100 bill back and got full credit.

– Submitted by Chet Miskel

Sale #3

Ask and You Shall Receive

LEARNING LESSONS FROM THE FIELD

During my second year in the mortgage-banking business, I was transferred to a new territory with tremendous growth potential. The transfer rewarded me for setting new company sales records in a difficult and limited market.

As a loan representative, I earned a commission for each new home loan originated for my employer. My primary duties required calling on real estate companies, builders and developers – mostly real estate salespeople.

Since my company specialized in FHA and VA lending programs, I selected real estate firms known as my market's top FHA and VA sales producers. I developed a sales strategy that included four main features:

- weekly sales calls to potential customers,
- rate sheets and program information for each sales agent's desk,
- scheduled telephone follow-up with each sales agent, and
- promotional mailings.

One real estate firm became my target account and I made a point of being in that office every Monday, Wednesday and Friday. Very soon I was on a first-name basis with everyone in the office and was invited to all of their meetings and social gatherings. I was now part of the family. What could be better?

One morning during my target customer's weekly sales meeting, the firm's most successful sales agent, whom I had come to know quite well (I knew her children's names, ages, the schools they attended – most of the things that friends know about each other), jumped up from her chair and exclaimed, "I need to call Bob Blank at XYZ Mortgage for a loan quote." Bob was an experienced loan representative whose company enjoyed an excellent reputation as the area's premier lender.

She reached for the phone and quickly dialed my competitor's number as I just sat there for what seemed like an eternity feeling stunned, foolish and embarrassed. Then I thought, this must be a joke.

Suddenly, the agent's face turned bright red. She put her hand over the mouthpiece of the telephone receiver, slowly raised her head and, looking directly at me, said, "Oh, I'm sorry. Aren't you in the lending business?" Still in shock, I remember nodding and stammering, "Yes. Yes, of course."

She hung up the telephone, gave a nervous little chuckle and said, "Let's get together after the meeting."

I not only closed the sale, but also learned a valuable lesson that day. No matter how often you call on an account, or how well you know your customer, always ask for the order! It's no fancy, state-of-the-art sales technique, but it can make the difference between closing and losing. – *Submitted by Thomas Kranig*

Sale #4

Getting Past Gatekeepers

HOW TO BREAK THROUGH AN INVISIBLE WALL

Before I became a business forms distributor, my wife and I were professional mimes. We toured 11 months a year, performing for two years on Caribbean cruise ships and in every state east of the Rockies. After 10 years of a grueling schedule, my wife and I decided to settle down and start a family, and I began my selling career. One company in my territory had a receptionist who was particularly talented at screening out cold-callers. I had stopped by several times and she wouldn't give me the name of the appropriate buyer or even take my card. No one could get past her.

> **I proceeded to build an imaginary wall around her desk. I went around her desk several times until I found a knob, opened the door and walked in and handed her my card.**

One day, since I had nothing to lose, I decided to try something different. Once again I approached her and she responded with the usual contemptuous stare. I then said, "I get a feeling that something is coming between us." With my gift of mime, I proceeded to build an imaginary wall around her desk. I went around her desk several times until I found a knob, opened the door and walked in and handed her my card.

She looked at my card, then looked at me and broke into a roaring laugh. She immediately phoned the buyer and, between giggles, demanded that he come right out to her desk. She made me tell him what happened, and then I performed my routine for him.

He loved my performance and set up an appointment with me for the next day!

He became a loyal customer and I only have one problem left. Each time I go there the receptionist asks me to do a little something. I've almost used up my repertoire.

– Submitted by Micah Bertin

Become a friend to every gatekeeper

Gatekeepers can help open doors – when you know how to use the right keys. Eileen Brownell, president of Training Solutions, offers the following tips on turning gatekeepers into door openers.

1. Keep your sense of humor. This is very important, Brownell says. If you can't laugh, your job will be much more difficult.

2. Be friendly and outgoing. Do the same for gatekeepers as you do for decision makers. Strike up a conversation and learn their likes, dislikes, preferences, what their kids do, if they have pets, whatever. Even over the phone you can tell a lot about people. This is valuable information you can use to help develop rapport with every person you meet.

3. Follow up. Make yourself memorable by making gatekeepers feel special. Send them a box of chocolates if you know they have a sweet tooth. If you see an article about the kind of pet they have and you think they might enjoy it, send it.

They'll appreciate that you made an effort to remember them. Such efforts can lead to a more relaxed atmosphere and will help you get through to the decision makers more easily.

4. Send thank-you notes. No one writes thank-you notes anymore, Brownell observes. After a visit send gatekeepers a nice note with your business card enclosed. This makes a wonderful impression and will open doors.

Eileen Brownell
Training Solutions

Sale #5

My Sales Gamble

AN ACE IN THE HOLE

Many salespeople send out product samples through catalog distribution and never follow up in person. My product, Queensland Opal Belt Buckles, was not exactly a major item for catalog distribution, so I knew I would have to rely on showmanship if I hoped to get in the door – let alone close the sale.

I decided to start at the top – the president of one of the largest mail-order houses in Texas. After anonymously confirming with the president's secretary that he would be in the office the Friday I planned to make my presentation, I did not make an appointment, but decided to gamble.

At the secretary's desk I whipped out my next playing card and announced, "Please tell Mr. Zale that the Ace of Hearts is here to see him."

On Monday, for Tuesday delivery, I express mailed a playing card, the jack of hearts, to the president – no note, no letter, no business card. On Tuesday, for Wednesday delivery, I express mailed the queen of hearts – again, no note, no letter. On Thursday, I express mailed the king of hearts to the president. Then on Friday, with my heart pounding, I approached the president's office. At the secretary's desk I whipped out my next playing card and announced, "Please tell Mr. Zale that the ace of hearts is here to see him." Even before she picked up the intercom receiver, Mr. Zale had bounded from his office dying of curiosity to see what the "ace of hearts" looked like and who the person was behind those unusual messages.

I greeted him with genuine enthusiasm and said, "Just as I have captured your attention, my product can do that and more." I went on to say that to put an end to all this mystery, why not sit down and take a look. I presented my product. He escorted me to his buyer and announced, "I want to do business with this lady." The company placed a large order that day – an order previously unheard of in the industry. This became a long and steady account.

My winning sale proves the more creative and innovative the sales presentation, the more genuine the enthusiasm of the prospect and the more sales closed. – *Submitted by Donna O'Dunn Wick*

Sale #6

Know Your Competition

BEAT THE COMPETITION

"Beat the Competition." This axiom went along with the sign over my desk that admonishes, "If nobody ever sells, nobody eats." Competition was very much on my mind as I set out to respond to a call from a subsidiary of one of my major competitors. My task: to provide an enhanced operating system for my competitor's mainframe computers.

Armed with a slide presentation and sufficient literature for 50 percent more than the anticipated 10 people, I planned a standard 90-minute presentation of my very complex subject. The interest level was high, mainly because the home office of my potential customer – which was supplying the operating system – was not responding to this company's problems or to requests for improvements.

As the attendees came into the room I introduced myself, noted their names and functions and asked them frankly what difficulties they were experiencing and what they felt they needed. As the presentation began – to double the number of attendees expected – I warmed to my subject and began pointing out specific benefits to members of the group to meet their specific difficulties and needs, all the while reinforcing my points with success stories and references. They began to be drawn in, and questions and explanations grew. The coffee wagon and lunch cart came by and left, and no one made a move because they didn't want to miss anything.

When we finally tied things up after four hours, I was exhilarated. I had made not just another sale *over* the competition, but a sale *to* the competition! *–Submitted by Sam Holland*

Sale #7

Limitless Opportunities

DON'T MISS THE BUS

A delinquent school bus helped bring me my very first sale as a voice mail and auto attendant salesperson and proved that profitable selling situations are everywhere if we keep our eyes open.

Soon after beginning my sales career, I was awaiting my first grader's school bus one afternoon, but the bus simply never arrived. I drove home and called the local school board district office to inquire where the bus was. All of my calls were either unanswered or met with a busy signal. I had even begun to wonder if the office had taken the phone off the hook, when the bus finally arrived.

My professional experience told me that the office had an overextended switchboard. Never one to overlook an obvious

---

Wow your customers unexpectedly

Giving customers what they expect won't build loyalty. You have to give them what they don't expect, says speaker, trainer and author Jeffrey Gitomer. To take your buyers by surprise and earn their lifelong loyalty, never pass up these golden opportunities.

Make a positive first contact. Your initial customer greeting sets the tone for everything else. That first contact with the customer is your first shot at "Wow!"

Recover when things go wrong. Mistakes give you a chance to recover in a memorable way. You can offer a stupid, lame defense excuse or you can say, "You know what? That's my favorite problem. When something like this happens it makes me totally ecstatic because I get to blow you away with something cool."

Respond after the sale. When I threw my back out for the first time in my 53-year life, I called a chiropractor – on a Saturday. On Saturday night he called me back and told me to come in the next day. On Sunday I was his only patient and he fixed my back. Wasn't that enough? He didn't stop there. He called me Sunday night to see how I was – and this man is the most successful chiropractor in Charlotte, NC, not someone desperate for business.

Jeffrey Gitomer
BuyGitomer Inc.

opportunity, I contacted the school board's purchasing department the following day to set up a sales appointment.

Before the appointment was over I had convinced the department it needed an auto attendant and voice mail system to install a hotline. The hotline would allow parents with inquiries about late buses to call and enter a bus number to find out about any delays. I illustrated the department's need for the hotline by conveying the panic I felt when I was unable to learn the whereabouts of my child's bus.

Not only did I sell the much-needed system to our own school district, but several nearby school districts followed suit and installed the system.

I have applied what I learned from this situation throughout my sales career. All obstacles, personal and professional, present opportunities if you'll only recognize them. – *Submitted by Chris Pool*

Sale #8
Selling with a Personal Touch
IF YOU GET LEMONS...

For more than a year's worth of sales calls, I could always count on Bill for a friendly but unproductive appointment. Though I knew his company did a lot of printing, he simply wasn't placing any orders with me.

As an ex-smoker, Bill kept a bag of lemon drops in his desk to help curb his craving for a cigarette. While I was in his office one day, he pulled out the bag, offered me a lemon drop, then took one himself – the last one, I noticed. That particular visit was no different from the rest – I left with yet another cordial contact but no sale.

When I got back to town, though, I stopped at a candy store. Knowing Bill had eaten his last lemon drop that day, I purchased 10 pounds of lemon drops, packaged them and shipped them to Bill to arrive the very next day. Ten pounds of lemon drops is a considerable bundle, and for what I was making in those days it was a pretty extravagant gesture. And also one of the smartest moves I ever made.

Knowing Bill had eaten his last lemon drop that day, I purchased 10 pounds of lemon drops, packaged them and shipped them to Bill to arrive the very next day.

The next day Bill called to say, "In all my years nobody ever did anything like that for me. You get over here tomorrow morning."

"But," I protested, "I was just there yesterday."

"Makes no difference," he said. "Be here at 10 o'clock."

Needless to say, I was there at 10:00 a.m. and got the biggest printing order I'd ever sold – the first of many from Bill. He eventually became my number one customer. For the price of a box of lemon drops and overnight shipping, a previously fruitless calling pattern turned into a sale I'll never forget. It had little to do with lemon drops, of course, and everything to do with being thoughtful, conscientious and creative. Human touches like this in an age of depersonalization (voice mail, answering machines, automated service lines) can create a bond between a salesperson and a customer that no competitor – even one with a lower price – can break."

– *Submitted by Bob Westenberg*

Sale #9

Giving All You've Got

I'LL BLEED FOR A SALE

I was on a five-day tour to a newly formed sales growth region as vice president for Craig Transportation, a multiregional trucking company. My first sales call was late. Consequently, for the rest of the day, I was late for every call.

Driving to the last stop of the day, I was a solid 20 minutes late to a promising account at a Baltimore-area bleach plant. To make

To this day my customer still recounts the story of the salesman so desperate to make up for lost time that he donated blood to keep the appointment.

matters worse, my cellular phone lacked service for the area. If I had stopped to call the prospect, I would have arrived even later. So I forged ahead.

When I finally arrived at the plant, I discovered that my prospect had left his office for somewhere else in the building where a company blood drive was in progress. The plant had set a goal for record donations.

So what else could I do? I quickly volunteered. After giving me the obligatory questionnaire, a nurse escorted me to a cot where I stretched out right next to my customer's cot. While we both dripped through tubes into our blood bags, I had my prospect's undivided attention for nearly an hour. To this day my customer still recounts the story of the salesman so desperate to make up for lost time that he donated blood to keep the appointment. Today this customer represents nearly $5 million in annual revenue. Sometimes it's good to pay in blood.

– Submitted by Christopher Simmons

Sale #10

Competitive Bidding

NEVER PASS UP AN OPPORTUNITY TO QUOTE

It was the early 1980s and I was an account manager in corrugated-paper packaging in eastern Pennsylvania and southern New Jersey. A former customer called and asked if I'd be interested in quoting on a million-unit lot of corrugated die-cut trays to hold 12-ounce soda cans.

"Sure!" I replied enthusiastically and set up an appointment. To my surprise, the quote turned out to be for a business acquaintance of my former customer who was now a consultant to the first high-speed soda canning operation in, of all places, Saudi Arabia.

Outbid the lower-cost competition

When you're the high-end product and you face a price-only buyer, apply these tips from Andrea J. Moses, director of Powerbase Performance Group, for outbidding the lower-priced competition.

Offer superior understanding of the customer's problem. Then counter with a superior solution to the competition's offer.

When the prospect reads your proposal, give three reasons why you are the only answer to the customer's problem.

Do thorough research and present solutions. Emphasize total value. Prepare surveys or scenarios which clearly show the cost of the problem, the cost of not taking action, the real cost of choosing a lower-cost solution and how much money the customer will save during a certain amount of time by investing more in your product.

Don't give the prospect the opportunity to bargain. Never fall into the trap of breaking down the components you are quoting, Moses advises.

That gives the customer the opportunity to nickel and dime the price.

Keep your competition in mind. Know your customer is comparing your product or service to your competitors'. You cannot simply say, "Ours is better." List 10 or 20 products and cost them out, showing how your product pays for itself over time and actually saves the customer money.

Andrea J. Moses
Powerbase Performance
Group

Somewhat skeptical, I worked up a quote as I had been doing for close to 20 years in industrial sales. I did extra homework to come up with the freight involved in the 4,000-mile delivery. After the quote request was completed and telexed to the foreign prospect, I spent the next two months servicing existing beverage, agri-business and manufacturing accounts and soliciting new business in my Mid-Atlantic states territory.

I found out firsthand never to pass up a chance to quote. It has led to unexpected foreign travel and subsequent business opportunities.

At the end of two months, a telex arrived announcing the bid had been accepted and placing the first order. A certificate of deposit, covering the first million units plus the land and ocean freight, was enroute. Suddenly I was involved in international accounts!

Success with the first account in Saudi Arabia led to a total of five accounts there and in the United Arab Emirates over the next two years, with a total of 33 million units sold.

Soliciting and servicing these accounts resulted in my traveling to England, Germany and Saudi Arabia, while still maintaining sales in my original U.S. territory.

I found out firsthand never to pass up a chance to quote. It has led to unexpected foreign travel and subsequent business opportunities not only with Saudi Arabians, Germans and English, but also Chinese and French business people!

– Submitted by Paul Garrison

Sale #11

Give Up? Never!

THE FLIMSY BUSINESS CARD

One of my most memorable sales occurred about 10 years ago while I was working for IBM as a marketing representative in Portland, OR.

Other salespeople had warned me about Mr. Smith (not his real name). He didn't like salespeople and enjoyed making them look like fools when they came to call. But, he was the president and owner of the company and if a sale of capital equipment (computers) was going to be made Mr. Smith would have to approve it.

As I entered the front door I could see Mr. Smith in his office. I announced to Mrs. Jones, the receptionist and Mr. Smith's secretary, who I was and that I would like to have no more than 10 minutes of Mr. Smith's time. I smiled and handed her my card. She answered coolly that she would inform Mr. Smith that I wished to see him.

Undaunted, I asked Mrs. Jones if I could borrow her stapler...If Mr. Smith was going to tear my card in two again, he was going to have to work at it.

She took my card into Mr. Smith's office and closed the door. A moment later the door opened and Mrs. Jones returned. She handed back my card, which had been torn in half, and said sadly, "Mr. Smith didn't say anything but I don't think he wants to see you today." Undaunted, I asked Mrs. Jones if I could borrow her stapler. As she watched, I stapled my card back together with three neat staples down the middle. Then I ran a row of staples around the outside edges of the card so that each staple just overlapped the previous one. If Mr. Smith was going to tear my card in two again, he was going to have to work at it.

Again I asked Mrs. Jones to announce my presence to Mr. Smith. I promised not to take more than 10 minutes of his time, and I asked her to extend my apologies to Mr. Smith because I had such a flimsy calling card. With a slight smile and a twinkle in her eye, she took my stapled card into Mr. Smith and closed the door.

When the door opened again Mr. Smith emerged, holding my stapled card and chuckling. "You from IBM?" he bellowed. "Come on back – you've earned your 10 minutes."

Over the course of several more appointments, Mr. Smith purchased a computer for his company and became one of my best customers. The day the computer was delivered I brought Mrs. Jones a rose in a bud vase. – *Submitted by Robert Z. Wilkinson*

Sale #12

Don't Take No for an Answer

THE BUSINESS CARD MESSAGE

After reading "The Flimsy Business Card" in your Most Memorable Sale column, I was inspired to write about my own business card tale.

Several years ago, I was representing a printing and publishing house. There was a jobber, Mr. Riley, who was well known for his inaccessibility. "Oh, he's a hard nut to crack," the other salespeople warned me. But my company was producing a special line I felt certain would do well for him, so I decided it was worth a try.

Because he employed only a few people, he and his workers were always traveling. Consequently, the only chance to catch him in his office was on Saturdays. Although other salespeople had not even gotten in to see him, much less talk to him, I set out that weekend determined to see him, talk to him and sell him.

Before entering his building, I called to be sure he was in. When a clerk, in a moment of unguarded candor, told me he was there, I immediately entered his office and presented my card to his receptionist.

"He's not in," she told me. But I informed her that she or someone else had just told me he was there. She shrugged her shoulders and took my card into her boss's office.

She returned almost immediately and stated that Mr. Riley did not wish to see me. "Please tell him that I have a very special line to show him," I requested.

With a show of obvious reluctance, she went back into his office, only to return with my card. On the back was the message, "Too busy to be bothered."

For a moment, I didn't know what to do next. Then I had a brilliant idea. Drawing a line through his message, I neatly wrote, "What would you say if one of your own salespeople gave up now?"

It took quite a bit of persuasion to convince the receptionist to enter Mr. Riley's office again, but she finally relented, left my card on his desk and came back out without saying a word.

A minute later he called her and asked her to show me in. His first words were, "Young man, I'd say he was a quitter – now let's talk business."

My first order wasn't a big one, but I later received several large orders from this "tough nut." – *Submitted by Alfred B. Miles*

Sale #13

Providing Customer Service
MY CUSTOMERS COME FIRST

I was fresh out of college, and my first sales job was in a small advertising agency. I would listen to the radio to see who was advertising, then pay them a visit to determine if they could use my advertising agency's services.

One day as I was driving, I heard a grand-opening commercial for a local car wash and the next day met with the owner/operator of what turned out to be a small car wash.

Tom was a rough-looking character – unshaved and dressed in a worn flannel shirt and ragged jeans. He had already spent his advertising budget and didn't have any immediate plans to use additional funds.

Since I was hungry for any type of business, I made a point of stopping by to see Tom when I was in his area. One day he asked me if I could print up some new business cards for him. Although there was no money in this order, I did it anyway. A few weeks later he asked if I could help him design a new sign for his business. I did, and the job turned out well.

A couple of months went by and I continued to call on Tom every few weeks just to see if there was anything I could do for him. During that time I developed a great relationship with him. He always offered to wash my car for free because he felt bad for not giving me much business for the effort I kept putting into coming up with ideas for him. I told him I was happy to help him in any way I could to make his business more successful.

One day I got a call from Tom. He said his brother managed a couple of stores and might benefit from my services and that I should give him a call. Tom's brother, Jake, was a well-dressed, articulate businessman who managed several licensed departments inside major department stores. Jake spent so much on advertising that he easily could have become our small agency's largest account.

After determining Jake's needs and matching my agency's services to his needs, I was able to persuade him to let me handle all of his advertising. This was a major sale. Everyone at the agency was ecstatic and my sales numbers quadrupled overnight.

A year or so into our working relationship, Jake told me his brother Tom owned the whole operation and that he, Jake, was working for him. Jake added that by servicing Tom so well without knowing the full scale of his wealth, I had proved my value and commitment to him and his business. Without realizing it, I had won his trust and respect and learned a valuable lesson.

– Submitted by Randall S. Rozin

Sale #14

Accentuate the Positive Points
STRESSING THE BENEFITS

Early in my sales career I learned the importance of emphasizing the benefits of a product. I also learned to look for benefits in the product that were not always obvious.

The department store where I was employed stocked a variety of merchandise including lawn furniture. Early one spring, the store manager made a special buy on a truckload of folding aluminum chairs with plastic webbing. Unfortunately, the chairs didn't match any of the other lawn furniture and no one seemed interested in buying them.

So, I pulled a supply of the chairs from the warehouse, mass-displayed them and attached a sign that read, "Fishing Chair – $6.95."

When it began to look as though we would be stuck with the chairs, our boss said he wanted us to sell them, even if we had to mark them down below cost. Before we had an opportunity to reprice them, my dad happened to stop by the store and noticed the chairs.

"I've got a chair just like those," he said. "Makes a great seat when you're fishing from a muddy creek bank."

Suddenly, I had an inspiration. I knew there were hundreds of retired and semiretired people in our town who spent a lot of hours fishing in the nearby creeks and ponds. So, I pulled a supply of the chairs from the warehouse, mass-displayed them and attached a sign that read, "Fishing Chair – $6.95."

In two days, the chairs were gone – and they were sold at our regular retail price. – *Submitted by Richard Thorpe*

Sale #15
Closing With Flair
NOTHING TO LOSE

Years ago I was out on my first call selling Filter Queen vacuums to a perfect stranger. As the young woman invited me in, her husband, a bowling bag in his hand, swooshed past me toward the door saying, "Honey, don't buy anything!"

Amazingly, the words seemed to calm me. It was as though the words helped make up my mind that this was only going to be another practice. I now felt I had nothing to lose.

Through the entire two-hour presentation to the woman and her best friend who was visiting, I was able to get her to ask questions and to get her to answer my questions positively. I was even starting to believe I could sell this lady a Filter Queen! After I had wrapped it up with our usual, impressive suction demonstration, I closed by asking, "Would you prefer to keep this machine, which is new except for this demonstration I just gave, or do you prefer I bring in a boxed one from my car?"

She said she'd take this one, but she didn't know how she'd pay for it. I then suggested our charge plan, which would cost only pennies per day. While her credit was approved, she'd have full use of the machine. And she had three days in which to change her mind and cancel the order if she wasn't delighted with the vacuum. Well, she took the machine!

Almost as an afterthought, I looked her friend in the eye and calmly asked, "Would you prefer the credit arrangement, also?" I knew she'd say yes, and she did. – *Submitted by Randal J. Logan*

Sale #16
Writing Better Sales Letters
A POWERFUL SALES ALLY

A number of years ago I wrote a solicitation letter to a senior executive at a national trade association describing a program to place him or his group's spokesperson on radio and TV programs in a broadcast publicity campaign. On my first follow-up call to the prospect, I reached his secretary who informed me her boss was "in a meeting, with his door closed."

I didn't need to be a Sherlock Holmes to deduce that both my letter and I would be filed away in a matter of minutes.

When I asked about a good time to talk with the boss, she told me he would be tied up all day and would be going on a trip the next day.

"I'll show him your letter," she said, "and if he doesn't get back to you, then you can assume he's not interested." I didn't need to be a Sherlock Holmes to deduce that both my letter and I would be filed away in a matter of minutes.

I quickly shot back, "But ma'am, I'm offering him the chance to obtain radio and TV exposure for your association and get the same visibility you've been getting with your present commercials – at a lower price!"

There was a pause and then the secretary said, "Well, I'll see if he can be interrupted." Moments later she returned saying that she had seen her boss and he had asked her to take my number to call me back.

About 40 minutes later, the phone rang. It was the prospect himself. Yes, he was interested in what I had to say. Ten minutes later I had an appointment. A week later I had a new client.

Perhaps the appointment and new business would have come anyway, just on the basis of my initial pitch letter. However, enlisting the understanding and active support of the executive's secretary bought me a few valuable points and helped streamline the whole new-business solicitation process.

– Submitted by George Haber

Sell the write way

Powerful and convincing sales letters often lead to follow-up calls that reach the decision maker. Brody Communications president Marjorie Brody offers these tips for action-oriented, benefit-focused letters that will help you write your own ticket into your buyer's office.

1. Why are you writing? Keep in mind your objective and your audience, and ask yourself before you start, "What do I want as a result of the letter? What do I want the people to know, do or feel as a result of getting this letter?" Don't leave your readers wondering, "What am I supposed to do with this? Am I going to hear from you? Do you want me to call you? Do you want me to send something back?"

2. You sell in benefit terms, and your letters should be written in benefit terms. Brody explains that salespeople need to tell customers clearly in their letters what the benefits, not the features, of the product or service mean to them.

3. Don't write beyond the level of your audience. Watch your use of large words or pretentious language and pay attention to acronyms, jargon and buzzwords. Keep your tone conversational – write for the ear, not the eye.

4. Be proactive, not inactive; use active language, not passive language. Watch out for such power-robbing words as *try, hope, guess, think* and *maybe.* Use power words: *urge, recommend, suggest.*

5. Review and proofread. Always put your material down and look at it a day later for content. Proofread to avoid mistakes. Prospects pick up on sloppy work, which reflects on the salesperson.

6. In general, shorter is better. However, if your letter is a good read and presents good value, people will keep reading it regardless of length.

Marjorie Brody
Brody Communications Ltd.

Sale #17

Winning Back Lost Customers

NO PAIN, NO GAIN

When a customer stopped buying our products due to our poor lead times and questionable product quality, I made it my duty to win her back. As the product manager, I knew very well the improvements we'd made since this customer's bad experience. On my initial call to her I addressed the quality and delivery issues at length, reassuring her that I would handle her account personally. I followed up that call with several more, each time trying to reassure, explain and progress to the next step.

I wasn't new to comments, questions, objections or rejection but this insult caught me off guard.

On my tenth call or so on this customer she told me in no uncertain terms that I was becoming a real pain. I wasn't new to comments, questions, objections or rejection but this insult caught me off guard. Nevertheless, I chuckled diplomatically and told my customer that I wouldn't give up that easily.

True to my word I kept calling, and about four months after my initial call my customer decided to place the first of what would become many orders. She now calls me with more orders, questions, comments and sometimes just simple conversation, and our business with her has grown by 86 percent this year. By being persistent and keeping our name in front of this customer, her pain turned into everyone's gain!

– Submitted by Brett T. Snow

Sale #18

Creating the Right Presentation

A DIRTY JOB AND IT WAS ALL MINE

I landed my most memorable sale on a hot and windy day...smack in the middle of a garbage dump.

A new rep and I were on a particular call as part of his training. I let him handle the presentation by himself while I remained in the car. As I was waiting, I noticed one, then two, then three – an entire parade of dump trucks – passing back and forth. I noted the company name painted on the side of the trucks and, upon closer inspection, I found that we had not called on that firm yet – nor were they even listed in the phone book.

When the new rep came back to the car, he asked, "Well, where to next?" I answered, "See that truck coming up the street? Follow it, wherever it goes!" And off we went.

After trailing the convoy of dump trucks for seven miles, we arrived at its final destination – a very odorous, sanitary landfill. I looked around and noticed at least 50 vehicles and 11 buildings, plus so many employees you couldn't tally them all. Since our sales prices are based upon the number of employees, I knew I had a big selling opportunity in this heap of rubbish. I asked an employee to direct me to the head of the business – fully expecting him to lead me to one of the several office-type buildings scattered in front of me. Instead, the corners of his mouth turned upwards into a wide, toothy grin and he pointed toward the middle of the landfill. About 100 yards in front of me a large, loud bulldozer was digging in the muck, with my prospect in the driver's seat. With a sadistic chuckle, my director said, "If you want to talk to George, you have to go to him. He don't come to you."

After trudging through shin-deep mud and rubbish, I made my sales presentation – perched on the rails of the bulldozer in the middle of the landfill, yelling over the crescendo of dozer noise, with perspiration pouring down my brow and amid unidentifiable trash blowing in the wind. When I closed, I had made not only an instant sale, but a landmark one. George, the man at the dozer's helm, wrote me a check, on the spot, for the largest amount I had sold for two months.

It was a dirty job, and I'm glad it was mine.

– Submitted by D. Neumann

Sale #19

Improving Listening Skills
USE YOUR PROSPECT'S NAME TO GAIN RAPPORT

As a regional training director, I work with sales representatives having all levels of experience. In one of my basic selling skills courses I discuss effective listening as well as using the customer's name in a conversational manner when making a sales call. I often tell this story from my own sales experience to shed light on both these important skills.

While making a call one day, I came upon a potential customer. After my initial contact, I set up an appointment for the following week to make my presentation and close the sale. As I got into my car and was jotting down some notes, I tried to recall the customer's last name. He was a petite man in stature. Ah ha! I remembered I had sought the help of a mnemonic device. Because the man's name was Small and he in fact was petite in size, it was easy to recall!

When I returned the following week to close my sale, I sat in Mr. Small's office. During our final conversation, I was carefully explaining the finer points of my new system to Mr. Small. "You'll be glad to know, Mr. Small, that this system will not only save you time, but also money. Mr. Small, this will allow you to reinvest the capital gained into your business to provide for further growth. Is this the kind of system you'd like to have working in your business, Mr. Small?"

At that moment, Mr. Small smiled and picked up my contract. As his eyes skimmed the finer print, with his pen in hand, he said, "I think you're right, Liz. This is the system we really need. By the way, just one more thing. My name is Short, not Small."

My point about proper use of a prospect's name and using good listening skills is quick to register with all new sales professionals.

— Submitted by Lisabeth B. Todd

Hearing and listening test

Assess your level of listening skills with these questions from speaker, trainer and *Investigative Selling* author Omar Periu.

Does your mind often wander while others speak to you? Focus on their words instead of thinking you've heard it all before. Buyers can sense when you've tuned them out and may refuse to buy when you close.

Do you often share your opinion on an issue before other people involved can share theirs? Wait. Listen patiently and gather your thoughts before speaking. Show consideration for the buyer.

Do VIP customers intimidate you so that you use their speaking time to plan just the right response? My dad always taught me that all people put their pants on one leg at a time. If you're nervous, take a nice deep breath to relax before presentations or sales calls on high-level executives.

When others speak about a subject on which you are an expert, do you feel compelled to speak up and share your knowledge? Even when your expertise exceeds your buyers' on a topic, let them dictate the pace of the sale. Then come back with a recommendation that shows you listened closely and understood.

Omar Periu
Omar Periu International

Sale #20

Add Variety to Your Selling

BETTER LATE THAN NEVER

I was one hour late for my most memorable sale and that brought me more than $1 million worth of business in one year. I was a successful kitchen cabinet salesman in the late 1950s, and in 1960 I was offered the challenge of building the territory of Staten Island for a major kitchen cabinet manufacturer in New Jersey.

When I drove up to the job site and approached the three sons, they all looked at their watches and chimed in unison, "You're an hour late."

After researching the builders on the island and finding out who was the largest and most influential, I set as my goal to sell this builder. This sale would not only bring me short-term success, but long-term rewards as well if I could use the builder as a reference on future calls to other builders.

My strategy was to stop at the builder's job site every Tuesday and Friday precisely at 1:00 p.m. for the first five weeks (10 visits). On every occasion I was greeted by his three sons, who later became friendly with me. After the five weeks and 10 visits at 1:00 p.m. sharp, I deliberately made my next call at 2:00 p.m. When I drove up to the job site and approached the three sons, they all looked at their watches and chimed in unison, "You're an hour late." At that moment I knew that my strategy had worked.

I felt that if they were aware I was an hour late, they were also aware that I had been calling on them at 1:00 p.m. for the past five weeks. They must have been looking forward to my arrival at 1:00 p.m. on the day I showed up at 2:00 p.m. That interest usually leads to an eventual sale. I didn't have to wait long – that day the builder gave me an order for 20 sets of kitchen cabinets. Through the use of their name as my account, I succeeded in selling to more than 85 percent of the builders on Staten Island and accomplished the nearly impossible feat of writing more than $1 million worth of business my first year on the island. For this achievement I received all sorts of acclaim from the newspaper (*Staten Island Advance*), the Staten Island Home Buyers Association and the firm for which I worked.

Selling psychology, the element of surprise and deviation from the norm are practices I have used and still use with extreme effectiveness. They all have played and continue to play a major role in my success and my company's continued growth.

– Submitted by Sy Lehrer

Sale #21

Cold Calls Yield Results

COLD CALLS ARE HOT STUFF

It was about 10 years ago, when I was still a new salesman in the advertising/promotion business, that I learned the real value of a cold call. I had tried very hard, without any success, to get in to

"Our Product Measures Up." Without any hesitation I pulled out my favorite specialty which was a thick Lucite ruler.

make a presentation to a large pharmaceutical company. One day while driving through a residential area, I spotted a small sign for this company in front of what looked like a mansion. I pulled over and went inside. The receptionist told me that, while their offices were under construction, the entire marketing department of the company I wanted to call on had moved temporarily into this building.

I asked if I could see the product manager for the company's largest drug product. She called him and he said he would see me in five minutes. Soon, in his makeshift office, I told him about Worldwide Specialty Sales and myself. He told me that the FDA had just required that he issue new guidelines for the drug and also that the new advertising theme was "Our Product Measures Up." Without any hesitation I pulled out my favorite specialty, which was a thick Lucite ruler. I told him we could paint the back of the ruler black and print the new guidelines on it. The front of the ruler would have the product name and new slogan. The ruler was a great tie-in for "measure up." As he handed me the printed guidelines he said, "Alan, if you can fit all this on that ruler, you have an order for 100,000 rulers."

Five days later the order was secured. Three weeks later I recommended we do the same design on an inexpensive vinyl ruler and received an order for 200,000 vinyl rulers to be given to nurses.

Do cold calls pay off? Well, what do you think?

– Submitted by Alan Goldstein

Loving the cold call

You can look forward to cold calling more when you believe in its benefits, according to Profit Builders president Keith Rosen.

1. Have a positive outlook. When it comes to cold calling, your outlook determines your outcome. If you think it's a waste of time, intrusive, annoying, manipulative or intimidating, that's what you'll experience each time you cold call.

2. Replace negative assumptions with healthier, more productive ones. For example, remind yourself: "Cold calling is informative – it tells prospects how to locate the product/service they need" and "Cold calling is a way to educate and serve people – it enables the salesperson to become a trusted resource, preventing prospects from buying the wrong product or service or using a company that may not effectively fill their needs."

3. Focus on the prospect. Consequently, the focus shifts from the salesperson's negative assumptions to the prospect and the value that can be provided. "When you choose to upgrade your current beliefs in a way that serves you and your prospects, you'll find the permanent solution to eliminating call reluctance and accelerating your success," Rosen says.

Keith Rosen
Profit Builders

Sale #22

Follow the Customer's Lead

SALE ON THE RUN

While still a fairly new sales rep, I carried a line that I believed would be perfect for a particular top-of-the-line store. I rehearsed my presentation about good mark-ups, product flexibility and compatibility with the store's position in the market.

I blocked his path, put the order in his one hand and my pen in his other, and said, "John, I really can't see you today." The owner was always in a whirlwind, doing 10 things at once – taking a phone call, rearranging something, hurrying over to reassure a customer. Every time I called on him we'd exchange greetings, but we never managed to be alone for more than five minutes before the inevitable interruptions would begin.

I'd call for an appointment in advance. "Fine," he would say, "See you on the 5th." Then I'd write just to confirm the appointment. Of course, as soon as I started my well-rehearsed presentation, he'd disappear, apologizing sincerely as his voice and his attention shifted to a more pressing issue.

One day I parked in front of his store and wrote up an order of those items I thought would best serve his needs. As I walked toward him, he greeted me in his usual rapid-fire fashion, brushing me aside as if I didn't exist.

I blocked his path, put the order in his one hand and my pen in his other and said, "John, I really can't see you today. I left my engine running, so if you'll just give me your approval on this, I'll be on my way."

For an instant everyone around froze. Then John raised his eyebrows, nodded his head, signed the order and instantly resumed his hectic pace.

Though I haven't had to use this approach since then, I learned that buyers, in addition to persistence, often respond to original and creative closes! — *Submitted by Charles Wilf*

Sale #23
Sell Quality, Not Price
NOT THE CHEAPEST, JUST THE BEST

About two years ago I received a call from a potential customer asking for a price quote for auto insurance. He wanted me to give it to him right over the phone. He said he was calling around and had about five quotes and was looking to buy the cheapest he could get.

We're generally not looking for customers such as these since they'll probably be shopping again in six months. While I was getting the quotation form, I asked the prospect a few questions about the car and its usage. I then asked him what he did for a living. Sometimes this can tell you about usage, too.

He said he worked for a gourmet chocolate company. I said, "That's amazing. I had no idea you folks had the cheapest chocolate in town." He replied, "We're not the cheapest." I asked, "Then why would anybody buy it?" He answered, "Because we're the best in town." I told him, "We're the best insurance agency in town, too." He then said, "Okay, I see what you mean. I'll see you Monday morning." And he did. — *Submitted by Jim Slavish*

Sale #24

What Your Customer Needs
SELLING IS NOT ORDER TAKING

As a financial representative for Home Fed Bank of San Diego, I evolved from being an order-taker to becoming a seasoned sales professional by understanding the difference between the two. Order-takers are limited because they allow the client to control the sales session – opening only the accounts requested and nothing more. Sales professionals guide clients through the sales session – listening, acknowledging, supporting and closing on not only what the client came in for, but also on products that fulfill client needs uncovered during the sales session. This really hit home for me one day about two years ago.

My client was thrilled and I felt great. I had done more than just sell him something – I had really filled a need for him.

It was almost time to lock the doors one Friday evening when a new client walked up to my desk. As he sat down, I simultaneously looked at my watch and asked him how I could be of assistance. When he said he needed to open a checking account, I went into automatic order-taker mode and, for a full five minutes, I went about my business gathering the necessary data and filling out the required forms. Suddenly I realized what I was doing. He had ordered a checking account and that's what I was about to give him. I didn't even know how much money he was planning to deposit, what kind of average balance he kept or even if he needed his funds to be liquid.

At that point I stopped what I was doing, took a deep breath and started over. I began talking to my client, asking open-ended questions in order to elicit information. It turned out the checking account was to be used as a holding account for the down payment on a new home. He'd need the money within a month, he said, so he couldn't invest in a CD. The amount? A mere $40,000! I could hardly believe he was planning to put that much money in a checking account at 5 percent interest.

Once I recovered, I told him about a high-yielding money-market account that we offer. With check-writing ability and the convenience of telephone transfers and ATM access, he could have the best of both worlds. My client was thrilled and I felt great. I had done more than just sell him something – I had really filled a need for him. And guess what? He sold his current home for a lot more than he anticipated so when he had an extra $50,000 to invest, whom do you think he called? Not an order-taker, but a real sales professional.

– Submitted by Maxine Goldstein

Questions produce results

Buyers may speak up or clam up depending on the way you word your questions. Try *Socratic Selling* author Kevin Daley's tips for asking hypothetical "fantasy questions" to open up close-lipped buyers and get the answers you need to sell.

Use conditional words. Construct questions using such words as *if, suppose, were to,* and *would* to show you're asking for information – not a commitment to buy.

You're not asking the prospect to be committed to you or your product. You're just thinking out loud. That's why conditional words work.

Leave yourself out of it. Avoid using the words *I* and *we* and any other specific references to yourself. Excluding yourself encourages unfettered thinking. On the other hand, if you say, "If you were to sign the order today, when would you want me to get my product there?" you may get a nega-

tive reaction from buyers who think, "Wait a minute. I haven't said you're going to be involved in this."

Don't mention your product. Mention your product only in generic terms. Your product name implies a commitment to be sold and it doesn't help to insert it too soon. Early on, buyers really are not trying to buy a product – they're trying to solve their problem.

Kevin Daley
Communispond Inc.

Sale #25

Persistence Pays Off

CREATIVITY AND DETERMINATION MAKE THE SALE

Many years ago, armed with a write-in lead for a set of 54 volumes of great literature, I called on a private boys' academy, ready to present my product. Ordinarily the school or college purchased the product and I had no reason to assume anything different in this case.

Soon, however, I learned that my write-in prospect was a student at the academy. He was from the Philippines and needed the extensive reference collection for his studies and private use. Before making the final purchase, the student called his father, who was then head of the Philippine government, for approval of the purchase and to arrange for the transfer of funds. He was instructed to call his aunt, who lived 200 miles away, to provide payment in advance.

The student knew his aunt would be apprehensive, so I suggested we both go to call on her. He asked for permission to leave the grounds but was refused by a school official. I suggested that we go anyway and he could put a dummy in his bed for bed check in case we returned late.

Several hours later we arrived at the aunt's private boarding school. By then it was late at night. She could not comprehend the urgency of the matter. Nevertheless, after I had sold her on the merits of the product, she paid cash for my prospect's set and also purchased a more expensive set for her school library. This double sale concluded at 1:30 a.m.

The student returned to his dormitory with no one aware that he had been missing most of the night. We both remained silent about the episode.

I have told this story of persistence at sales meetings and, in subsequent years, have heard it told by others in slightly altered versions. The story proves that obstacles in the path of a sale can be removed by using creativity and determination.

– Submitted by Charles W. Mathison

Sale #26

Don't Be Caught Unprepared

ALWAYS...BE PREPARED

I learned this lesson when I was an account rep for a credit-reporting agency. While my situation didn't turn into a disaster, it was funny and made an impression on me – one that has lasted. I made a cold call on a customer who was a vice president of a very large bank in Houston. I stopped by to tell him of a great new piece of equipment we had available.

After listening to my presentation, he said without hesitation that he would take not one, but three. Since this was quite an increase in his monthly cost and decisions such as this normally take some time, I was surprised – so surprised, in fact, that I realized I had only one contract with me. I had to excuse myself and run across the street to my car to get more contracts.

Since I have always prided myself on my professionalism I was very embarrassed. From that point on, I've always been prepared.

– Submitted by Debra Beasley

Sale #27

Getting Your Foot in the Door

SOLE OF A SALE

In 1992 I was an inspired but inexperienced salesperson at a small trade publication in Seattle. Our "headquarters" – which is really stretching the term – was a small office and we had virtually no travel budget. Thus, making a good impression on a large East Coast prospect presented quite a challenge.

When all of my phone calls went unanswered, I tried faxing, with no better results. At the end of my rope, I tried thinking out of the box to come up with an innovative, attention-getting solution that would finally get the prospect to notice me.

I went to a local shoe store that displays shoes by putting one on a rack, with the mate in the back room. They always end up losing

shoes and usually have a box full of strays to dump at the end of the week. I was able to get an expensive Italian shoe at no cost, which I then mailed to my client with a note that began, "Now that I have my foot in the door..." I also included a media kit and a sample copy of our publication. Though it may seem like a silly gimmick, it worked and turned into my first order from this prospect – the first of many, I might add.

When all else fails, putting some creative thought into your approach can make a difference when you total up your sales.

– Submitted by Carol Davidson

From "no-no" to "know-how"

Make contacts that work for you, advises Lynne Waymon, president of Waymon & Associates. Her networking tips can help avoid rejections and help get your foot in the door.

1. Don't make excuses. Never say, "I'm too busy," "I'm too broke" or "I'm too bashful." Instead, join at least two professional associations. Such groups can help you meet prospects and network with others in your field.

2. When someone asks, "What do you do?" don't simply give your name, rank and job duties. Tell about your many talents, or how you solved interesting problems. Stand out!

3. When someone asks, "What's new?" be prepared...to be spontaneous. If you weren't born with the gift of gab, prepare an "agenda" in your mind so your small talk is smart talk.

4. Ever forgotten someone's name? Don't say you're sorry. Try giving your name again.

Say, "Hello! I'm ___. We met last month." Or, say with enthusiasm and warmth, "Hi. I remember you. Tell me your name again."

5. Handing out business cards alone won't open doors. Have a reason first. When meeting a prospect, listen well and note what you have to offer. When you "listen generously" you don't need excuses for giving a business card – you have real reasons.

Lynne Waymon
Waymon & Associates

Sale #28

Show What You Know

SERVICE MAKES THE SALE

A Florida entrepreneur ready to invest $30,000 in a human resource company contacted me for information on the company's general business area, competition and potential income projections. As a business and market researcher, I usually handle such calls by offering a price quote, then waiting for the inquirer to call back. This time, I changed my approach.

"I'm not too familiar with this particular area," I told the prospect. "Let me poke around a bit and find out if I can help you."

Over the next few hours I did a quick data search, made a few phone calls to friends in the industry and concluded that I had access to information that the prospect would indeed find very valuable. Moreover, I believed he had stumbled on an exciting and potentially lucrative area.

I called back the following day and provided the prospect not only with specific information, but with encouragement that my research would be of great value to him.

"You seem to have a good handle on this," the prospect replied, "Let's do it." The prospect told me that although my price was actually 50 percent more than he'd expected to pay, he was so impressed with my findings that he felt my understanding of his needs put me far ahead of my competitors.

The risk of working without compensation was a small price to pay for the confidence my research inspired in the customer. By doing something to set myself apart from the competition, I made it easy for the customer to choose me. – *Submitted by George Haber*

Sale #29

Effective Qualifying
BIG SPENDERS HAVE NO UNIFORM

Two weeks after I got a job selling cars for the largest Chevy dealership in west Texas, a man walked into the showroom looking as though he had just come off an oil rig. The other salespeople must have thought he was looking for some used wheels or just killing time because this hot prospect got the cold shoulder from the other reps. Finally, the dealership's top producer passed him to me.

By this time the man was wondering why no one had taken him seriously enough to sell him a car. I, however, jumped at the chance. The scruffy-looking prospect turned out to be the president of one

---

Qualify prospects from the get-go

Avoid insurmountable objections down the road by qualifying buyers up front. Speaker, seminar leader and author Myers Barnes says you can be sure you have a truly hot prospect by covering these four qualifying bases.

1. Ask for wants, needs and desires. Start off by asking prospects, "What is it that keeps you awake at night? What's your greatest concern? What would you expect out of our relationship together? If you could describe the ideal outcome, what is it you'd like to achieve?"

2. Set a time frame. Variations in buying time frames can dramatically affect how you should follow up with prospects. Come right out and ask, "How soon were you planning on taking advantage of my service or someone else's service? What is your time frame?"

3. Seek authority. Buyers don't have to be decision makers to be decision breakers. To find out who has a say in the buying decision, ask who's actually going to use the product, who will cut the check and if there is anyone else who might be in the decision-making loop (third-party approval).

4. Identify a budget. Willingness to pay and ability to pay are two separate issues. Ask your buyers what they have in mind to pay for your product. That's what they're willing to pay. Next ask, "Up to?" Most of the time they'll give you a higher figure – closer to what they're actually able to pay.

Myers Barnes
Myers Barnes Associates Inc.

of the region's largest oil-drilling companies and had money to burn. I listened carefully to him and treated him like the valued customer he was, and the prospect no one wanted ended up buying two new pickups for his company and three Corvettes – one each for his wife, his son and himself. I made a commission of $6,000 and earned a $2,000 bonus for selling five cars. The lesson I learned that day remains for me the first law of sales: Don't prequalify prospects on superficial grounds. Prospects dressed in rags can still bring you riches. – *Submitted by Raj Madan*

Sale #30
Customer Appreciation
SHOW OF GRATITUDE

In an effort to diversify my personnel placement agency's client base, I set my sights on a major electric company. Unaware that this company had a long relationship with my local competition, I made cold calls with high hopes.

Finally, my calls paid off and the vice president of engineering agreed to meet with me the following week. To prepare for my appointment, I studied all the sales literature I could get my hands on, but I had one recurring thought – people want to feel appreciated. At the meeting, I told my prospect about our company and what we could do for him.

Unfortunately, the electrical industry wasn't our specialty and we didn't have a strong presence in the area. I sensed that I was losing the battle, so I looked my prospect in the eye and said, "Sir, I am new to this industry but I really want to be a success. The only way to do that is to earn it and there is nobody out there who wants to earn your business more than I do. If you give us a shot, I will not let you down." A smile spread across my prospect's face, then he called his secretary in to take all of our pertinent information. He shook hands and told me to expect a contract in the mail and to call him personally if it didn't arrive within the next few days. I did call – not because the contract didn't arrive, but just to let him know how much I appreciated the chance to do business with him. Sometimes you can earn a prospect's business just by saying honestly how much it means to you. – *Submitted by Mike Forster*

Sometimes you can earn a prospect's business just by saying honestly how much it means to you.

Sale #31

Networking Skills

A FISH STORY

Although I conduct seminars in networking, I'd had no luck selling my services to the banking industry, where I thought my networking skills would pay off. After making calls to several prestigious banks without success, my enthusiasm was only lukewarm when I called on one mid-size regional bank. Still, I wanted to give it my best shot.

I pressed him for the whole story, and apparently made his day by giving him the opportunity to brag about his grandson's accomplishment. As I waited at the receptionist's desk, I noticed a huge rainbow trout hanging on a wall in a distant office in which an elderly gray-haired gentleman sat behind the desk. As I was scheduled to leave for my annual trout-fishing weekend the next day, the fish really caught my attention. When I met with the marketing director downstairs, she told me the fish belonged to the chairman of the board.

About two minutes into my presentation to the marketing director, I got a golden opportunity to speak with the chairman, who had come downstairs for a cup of coffee. After introducing myself to him I asked about the trout on his wall. He quickly corrected me with, "That's not a rainbow trout, it's a king salmon!" Then he told me that his two-year-old grandson had hooked it on a trip to Alaska several years ago. He told me that he'd made a deal with his grandson to mount the fish if the boy could reel it in. I pressed him for the whole story and apparently made his day by giving him the opportunity to brag about his grandson's accomplishment. After he finished his story, he said to the marketing director, "I like this young man. Whatever he is selling, you give him serious consideration." The marketing director then booked two seminar dates.

In this case my networking skills really paid off. I took the time to look for the individual interests of my potential buyer (or in this case someone with great influence on the buyer) and the little effort it took brought me one big sale. – *Submitted by Brad Hirni*

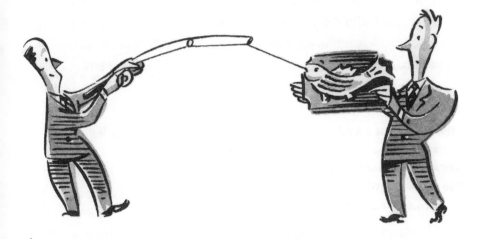

The right way to network

Professional events can yield big rewards. But not if you blow your chance by playing the fool. Consultant and trainer Barbara Pachter explains that successful networking requires knowing what not to do or say. You can learn from the mistakes of the six types of networkers who make the worst impressions.

1. The "there's-someone-else-I'd-rather-be-talking-to" people are willing to talk to you but keep looking around the room or at someone else.

2. The "terminators" are pushy types who crush hands during a handshake and invade other people's space.

3. The "nice-meeting-you-gotta-run" networkers are fast talkers who go through a box of business cards in a week but make no effort to establish meaningful business relationships with others.

4. The "fashion disasters" make a terrible impression – they dress too casually or wear dirty, wrinkled or ill-fitting clothes.

5. The "I-wish-this-wall-could-swallow-me-whole" types say it all with bad body language – arms folded across the chest, shoulders hunched, feet crossed at the ankles. These networkers don't talk much and seem uninterested.

6. The "I'm-the-greatest-thing-since-email" networkers love to hear themselves talk and are distracted and bored when they're not the center of attention.

Barbara Pachter
Pachter & Associates

Sale #32
Food for Thought
A BAKER'S DOZEN

During my years as a pharmaceutical rep, I had an assignment to land an account with the premiere physician in a town in my territory. The physician was responsible for writing the majority of prescriptions for a certain drug needed for recovering from orthopedic surgery.

Because he was so valuable to every pharmaceutical rep, he had been inundated with proposals and calls and was no longer seeing anyone representing any company that was not on his approved list.

The doctor came out with a half-eaten long john and asked who had forced him off his diet. Within 15 minutes I had a sale.

Since we were new in town, my company was not on that list. I never could get to see him through conventional methods.

Finally I began to spend time with the office receptionist and discovered that the physician had a real sweet tooth and was especially fond of a particular bakery specialty called a chocolate "long john." In fact, every morning he enjoyed one of these chocolate-covered treats made by a local bakery.

So I arranged with the baker to make a dozen long johns and write the name of my company's product on the top of each long john. I added a note about my product inside the box top. I delivered them to the doctor's office early in the morning before he began to see surgical patients.

Then I waited in the office. The doctor came out with a half-eaten long john and asked who had forced him off his diet. Within 15 minutes I had a sale. Our company went on to become very successful in that community. – *Submitted by John Oglesby*

Sale #33

Visualizing Yields Results

WORD PICTURES SOLD FOR ME

My most memorable sale came shortly after I joined a second-stage manufacturing start-up located on the Eastern Shore of Maryland. The many hours on the road enabled me to listen to a wide variety of training and motivation cassettes.

On one trip into central Pennsylvania I was listening to Zig Ziglar's cassette series, "Secrets of Closing the Sale," which addresses the issue of painting word pictures. It was a pleasant spring day when I came upon a little combination garage and car dealership. Using my Van Conversion Demonstrator, I made my presentation to the owner, who was clad in mechanics garb, oil on his pants and shirt. At what Mr. Ziglar might call the "right psychological moment," I asked the owner to picture a line of our van conversions in front of his store and to think about the extra profit he would realize by having our product. He began to stare at the curb in front of his shop but did not respond when I tried to close.

After what seemed like an eternity and having received no response, I asked again if he could picture the extra profits which our line could produce for him and asked if he could see the line of van conversions. Then the man, who was still staring at the curb in the front of his shop, put a wad of chewing tobacco in his mouth, turned to me and said, "No, son, I can't see that line of van conversions but I believe you can. I'll take the one you're driving, right here."

I left my Demonstrator by that curb and left his store by taxi. It was a most memorable sale for me. – *Submitted by Jeffrey A. Watters*

Sale #34

Establishing Rapport

PASSIVE PITCH?

For almost a year I'd been calling on the biggest prospect in my territory – a physician I knew would benefit from my services. The doctor had agreed to buy from me long before but never followed up with an order. Determined to keep trying, I returned to the office again and again, each time with new information that I'm sure ended up in the round file. The receptionists asked why I kept coming back when the doctor didn't want to see me. I told them my services would help him and his patients and that I thought he was denying the community a valuable and medically necessary service. I also said my manager would have a few choice words for me if I gave up, but my replies only seemed to strengthen their resolve to keep me out.

> After so much effort and preparation, when I finally went in as a friend, I lowered my buyer's resistance enough to get the order.

After playing this game for 11 months, I decided to leave my literature and sales pitch behind and stop in just to say hi and chat about anything but business. On my fifth such visit, the doctor walked in as I was talking to the staff. He remembered me, we started talking and within 15 minutes he asked who else used my services in the area and what my new fees were. Having deliberately left all my information behind, I had to excuse myself to go get it. The doctor gave me a trial test date the very next week and has been my best customer ever since. After so much effort and preparation, when I finally went in as a friend, I lowered my buyer's resistance enough to get the order. – *Submitted by Michael Norton*

Sale #35
The Power of Prayer
HEATING IT UP

I'd been on the show circuit for about five years, selling various products at state and county fairs and other large expositions all over the country. In September of 1982 I was selling electric quartz heaters at a county fair in my home state of Michigan. However, I was having a problem selling these heaters because of the warm and humid temperatures we were having.

I prayed for an answer and in a little while an interesting idea came to me. I decided to give away some Bibles with the heaters as a free gift. The next day, before the show started, I went to a publisher that sold Bibles wholesale and bought 50 paperback New Testaments. I then went back to the show and put a Bible inside each of the individual boxes that contained a heater. Amazingly, within a few hours time the temperature dropped down to the mid-50s, it became cloudy, started to rain and became windy and miserable outside. With that kind of weather, nobody wanted to stay outside on the midway for the rides. Most of the people rushed into the commercial building where my booth was located to get warm by my sample heater, which I had turned on to demonstrate. So many people bought my heaters that by the next day I had completely sold out the 50 heaters and was taking orders from my sample! The Lord had both honored my request to give away 50 Bibles and solved my problem of slow sales at the same time. The Lord caused the weather to be cool long enough to turn very poor sales into a great success!

– Submitted by Richard B. Hawkin

Sale #36

Overcoming Objections
NEVER GIVE UP

My job is selling motor club memberships to various types of prospects. We may call on bankers in the morning and plumbers in the afternoon. A salesman from another district who had been having problems selling had been assigned to me so that I could show him how memberships were sold.

We called on some of our appointments. Bad luck. Two prospects had suddenly been called out of town and another reluctantly arranged an appointment for later. To try a different approach, we started making cold calls on small businesses.

It was already afternoon and no sales. I decided we had better try another type of prospect. The rain was coming down hard and I was wet, chilly and unhappy because I had not been able to show the visiting salesman any sales. I was about ready to give up when I noticed a small store.

"Why don't we stop?" I said. We walked in. The owner was a big man. He looked like James Arness stalking a criminal in Dodge City. He was frowning down at me. I said with a big smile, "I'm from AAA and I would like to tell you about it."

"No," he said gruffly, "I'm not interested."

It was an old-fashioned country store with a potbellied stove. We walked dejectedly to the back and warmed up. Somehow I bolstered my courage and walked to the front where the owner was. "Mr. Owner," I said, "it's raining outside, you're not busy, you're not obligated, but could I tell you how the membership will benefit you?"

"Aw heck, go ahead," he said. I gave an enthusiastic demonstration using visual aids, asking questions as I told the story. The owner suddenly changed and became interested. He bought in less than five minutes.

"Follow me," the owner said. We went to the back of the store. The owner came over to the stove and brought another person with him. He said to the person, "Buy the membership, it's a good deal." He bought. This continued until everyone in the store bought. Some more people came in. They were introduced to me and they bought. Finally, one crusty old farmer was introduced to me but he didn't buy and started out the door. The owner followed him to the door and talked him into coming back. He bought.

The salesman with me was now convinced that people would buy the membership. We spent less than one hour in an old country store and sold 17 new memberships.

I still wince each time I think about how close I came to taking no for an answer and giving in to defeat. – *Submitted by Boyd Blanton*

Overcoming objections online

Although not everyone has email or access to the Internet, today's new technology allows you to showcase your products and services to prospective customers and eliminate possible objections, according to Thomas Wood-Young, president of Wood-Young Consulting.

Build trust and answer questions with a knock-out Web site. A superb Web site will have certain information to win prospects' trust – frequently asked questions (FAQs); information about the marketplace, product or service from the customer's point of view; and references, testimonials or comments from companies, with links to their Web sites.

Use email. Wood says the Internet allows gentle education – the customers are able to learn at their own pace. Email also allows customers to answer in their own time frame. "The Web and email let customers be in the driver's seat."

Stay top-of-mind. With the Internet and email it is possible to stay in constant contact with prospects without making appointments or driving all day. Even if they don't buy right away, prospects will remember you if you make the right impression. "If you have what it takes, and your Web site has the right 'punch,' the next time they place an order it might be with you," Woods notes.

Thomas Wood-Young
Wood-Young Consulting

Sale #37
Adding Value
THE SALE'S NOT OVER TILL IT'S REALLY OVER

When I was selling copiers, I had stopped a couple of times at a school in a town of about 10,000. On my third visit, the secretary told me that the old mimeograph that the school had been using "since the days before Columbus" had about had it and school offi-

Besides offering them a really good deal, I put things in perspective. cials were ready to start looking at copiers to replace it. After a qualifying interview, I brought in the appropriate unit to demon-

strate. School officials were impressed but said they would have to look around a bit before they committed.

Over the course of the next several weeks the school looked at maybe a half-dozen brands of copiers. I kept in touch, and after each demonstration or trial I assessed how ours stacked up. We stayed at the top of the heap until one company came in and tried to wrap up the sale by offering a ridiculously low price. I countered with the track record and features of my unit.

But my competitor came back with a new model with a dual-cassette option – something the school didn't really need.

The school hadn't given a final commitment to my competitor. I thought about possibilities overnight, and somewhere along the way I had an idea. I called the school the next morning.

I said, "If you really need two cassettes, and you're willing to pay $500 for that second cassette, I'll sell you my copier plus a good used copier for the price they're asking for their one machine. You'll have your two cassettes for the same price, and with this arrangement, you'll have a second whole copier attached to the other cassette."

That caught the school officials off guard. Besides offering them a really good deal, I had put things in perspective. Despite its being obvious, it hadn't occurred to them that that one feature would cost $500. A short time later I got the order – for the one copier. The school had decided that the second cassette wasn't really needed after all. – *Submitted by Lester M. Pope*

Sale #38
Gatekeeper as Customer
A GOOD EYE FOR A SALE

I am new to the contact lens industry but already have had a call I'll never forget. I was waiting to see an eye doctor and the receptionist took me into his office and asked me some questions about what products I had and how they compared to her boss's present choices. She asked me what I thought of what he was using, and I answered honestly that it was a good product.

I then proceeded to present the features and advantages of mine. She asked me how long delivery took, since everyone else said 24 hours. Based on her location I told her honestly it would take four or five days, but in a real bind I would try to borrow what she needed from another customer and bring it up in the next day or two.

After some small talk she asked for a price sheet to look at and then gave me a large order. The receptionist was in fact the doctor's wife, who runs this part of the practice – a fact unknown to many salesmen who had fluffed off her inquiries. She had selected his present product and knew deliveries to her were never in 24 hours! By not downgrading her present product, which was in fact a good one, and treating her like a customer before I knew she was one, I made a very nice sale. She has since reordered twice, and I have yet to say more than passing greetings to the doctor.

– Submitted by Richard Siles

Sale #39
Former Customers Aren't "Lost"
THE PRODIGAL CUSTOMER

After being hired to sell for a large construction supplies corporation, I was eager to prove myself. With all the enthusiasm of youth, I asked my new boss what lost customer he would most like to have back. He told me of a company that had severed its ties with us almost two years before. No one had been able to get them back, he said, and I shouldn't waste my time trying either. Determined to prove him wrong, I set out to meet the company owner. When I pulled into the construction site and asked for a moment of his time, he greeted me by saying, "God, I'm sick of salespeople!" Afraid I might crumble, I introduced myself. "Stop right there," he said upon hearing my company name. He explained that with my company he'd endured late deliveries, poor follow-up and a lack of attention to his company except when mine wanted an order.

> Even when your buyers are dissatisfied and disgruntled, determination and commitment to keep promises can help you win them over.

Hoping to make it up to him, I said, "If I promised on-time delivery and timely follow-up on each order would I have a shot?"

"Maybe," he said with a grin. We walked the job site discussing his needs and, although I said I would be back that week to pick up any order he would give me, he bought on the spot and I left with the order. Even when your buyers are dissatisfied and disgruntled, determination and commitment to keep promises can help you win them over. – *Submitted by John Boggs*

Sale #40

Going Above and Beyond

SOMETIMES A SALE JUST WALKS IN

A few years ago while working as a salesman at a prestigious furrier, I was in the store on a Saturday for security purposes. When the phone rang I answered it, and the caller asked for directions to the store. I told him the store was closed for the day. He said he would like to come in because it was his wife's birthday and he wanted to buy her a fur coat and they were already nearby after having traveled a considerable distance. I told the caller to come in and I would at least let him look at some coats.

When the caller and his wife arrived, I met them in the lobby. The gentleman agreed to stand near the front of the store and advise people we were actually closed, while his wife went into the store with me. As we entered the fur salon she saw a full-length mink coat on display and said, "I want that one." I put it on her and it fit perfectly. "I'll take it. How much is it?"

Pinch me, I thought. "That one is $6,500," I said.

"Great," she responded.

We went to show her husband and I said, "Your wife found a coat for dress; now we are going to find one for play." Would you believe she said, "Yes, that's a good idea." So, back we went and about five minutes later we found a beautiful fox coat that fit her perfectly. Again she said, "That's great, I'll take it."

Her husband came to the back of the store and I wrote up the sales – $10,500 with tax. He took out his checkbook and wrote out the check. When he said he wanted to take the coats with him, I thought, "Right, and Monday when we deposit the check it will bounce for sure." I told the man we would have to monogram the coats on Monday morning after which we would deliver them. "That will be fine," he said. He thanked me for going out of my way to be so helpful and they left the store.

Yes, it really happened this way. The check cleared the bank and this truly was the most memorable sale I ever made.

– Submitted by Bob Wilson

Sale #41

Tailor Solutions

INITIATIVE SELLS!

It was a slow Monday but I knew the sidewalk in front of my store would soon be full of working people going home. This daily rush usually didn't amount to added sales. On this day, however, I set a wide range of our fitness equipment out on the sidewalk. At five o'clock the waves began.

As I watched from outside the store, a man stopped in his tracks, peered in through the window, then proceeded inside. I quickly followed him in and, acting as if I were going to bring out more stock, asked if he had been helped. He said he hadn't, then indicated an interest in a fitness/weight machine for his office.

After developing a good rapport with him, I asked him why he was looking for a weight machine for his office. He told me he was an orthopedic surgeon and, unlike his colleagues, did not have an abundance of time to spare. He explained that he did not have a rehabilitation facility for his patients and had to monitor them at the local hospital, which was 45 minutes from his office.

The doctor said he needed a fitness/weight machine in his office so he could get the exercise he wanted without going to a health club, which he considered a waste of time and money. I took notes during the whole conversation. After asking for the dimensions of the room he was going to use, I set an appointment for the next morning.

That night I reviewed my notes and realized he could fit a large weight machine in the room with his other equipment, use the room for a rehab center and at the same time satisfy his personal needs. I carefully put together several floor plans, using a wide variety of weight and aerobic equipment, and called him to confirm our appointment.

The next morning we met and he loved my idea! With a few modifications of the floor plans, I closed the deal. Today we enjoy a great relationship and he has referred quite a few patients and friends to me. And all because I took the initiative! – *Submitted by Rick Early*

Irresistible offers

According to Kevin Davis, president of Kevin Davis Selling Systems, many salespeople go into presentation mode too soon. To make irresistible offers, ask the following questions.

1. What are my customers' buying criteria? Focus on customers' buying criteria from the beginning.

2. What's most important? How will your buyers measure the success of their purchase? Their answers will identify their dominant buying motive. Also, all criteria are not created equal. Don't ignore minor points of differentiation, especially in highly competitive markets.

3. Which criteria represent a potential threat to the sale? If what's important to your customer happens to be one of your offering's weaknesses, it's better to handle that sooner rather than later.

4. Which criteria represent my strengths? Learn to emphasize your strengths. Maybe there's something that's currently insignificant to your customer that you can make a case for to position yourself as a better choice.

5. Which additional criteria should my prospect be considering to achieve optimal results? Look at your most profitable customers and identify what their top 10 criteria were. What did they consider important that led them to buy from you?

Kevin Davis
Kevin Davis Selling Systems LLC

Sale #42

The Little Company Wins Big

WHALE OF A SALE

Almost three years ago I heard a sales training audiotape that advised me to "fish for whales and not minnows." Having recently switched positions from electrical engineer to eastern sales manager for a company providing maintenance and engineering services to power plants, I was inexperienced but decided to take the tape's advice and aim high. Our average contract value ($100,000) seemed like a minnow to me, so when I found a contract worth $18 million I jumped at the chance to win it.

First I convinced our purchasing manager that my company could handle the business; then I spent weeks writing a custom proposal.

First I convinced our purchasing manager that my company could handle the business; then I spent weeks writing a custom proposal. I addressed every buyer expectation from the request for a quote and even included a quote from the senior vice president on the benefit of specialized training that matched our training program.

My proposal earned me the chance to make a presentation, and although my competitors brought along their VPs and senior management, I brought only two project managers who had worked for the prospect company before and had connections I didn't. I explained to the buyer that we didn't need our senior management present because we would be accountable for our performance if we got the contract. The mammoth companies I competed against couldn't believe it, but I won the sale. They thought I cut our prices to buy the job, but the truth is I earned it by writing a proposal that gave the customers just what they wanted. My boss now calls me "The Bulldog" because once I sink my teeth into something I don't let go.

— *Submitted by Greg Cecchi*

Sale #43

The Importance of Integrity

I BEAT BACK A BUYER'S PRICE NEGOTIATION

One of the biggest thrills of my career came when a structural engineering firm chose my roof design, using our pre-engineered components, over competitive systems. It led to my biggest sale – $126,000!

Several months later their purchasing agent, Mark Olson, called. To this day I remember our conversation well.

MARK: Jim, as you know we have been awarded the contract for the project with your roof system. The bidding for the project was fierce. We bid low, perhaps too low. We're going to need all the help we can get from our materials suppliers and subs. What can you do for us on your $126,000 quote?

We bid low, perhaps too low. We're going to need all the help we can get from our materials suppliers and subs.

JIM (Taken by surprise and stalling to get my thoughts together): Congratulations, Mark, on your successful bid. It should be a fine project for all participating parties. Could you repeat your request for me? I'm not sure I understand but am ready to help if I can.

MARK: Jim, we all know that all quotes have some fat in them. We need you to review your figures and sharpen your pencil.

JIM: Mark, like your firm, I wanted this job badly. In order to bid structural integrity and still win over formidable competition, I had to keep my price low, perhaps too low. My policy has always been to give my best quote up front. That may box me in now and then, but I think you'll agree it's the only fair approach. (His voice revealed nothing, but he did thank me and said he would be in touch.)

He was – several more times in the weeks to come. His approaches varied but the aim never did. He was after a quote reduction.

One day he called with troubling news. He could beat my quote by more than $10,000 by substituting another truss. He would use my design with a truss inferior to ours.

Fortunately, I knew this substitute truss well – ours was head and shoulders superior. Unfortunately, product integrity and quality are often a hard sell to a low bidder. I immediately started working on a counteraction that hopefully would win for both of us.

Here is what I told him 48 hours later, "Mark, if the alternative approach you are considering was a sound one I would wish you well. However, I can't stand by and let you make a mistake that could jeopardize your firm's fine reputation with a possible structural failure and hurt your fine reputation as a purchasing agent.

"I have prepared for you an in-depth systems comparison showing the strengths and weaknesses of the two systems. All data have been reviewed and confirmed by our structural engineers and by the project's structural engineering firm."

One week later I was again in Mark's office, this time to accept and sign a purchase order for $126,000. I had successfully countered every one of his ploys and had managed to keep the sale intact.

– Submitted by Jim Worden

Sale #44

Make an Impression

FOLLOW-UP – IT'S A VITAL LINK IN MAKING SALES

About a year ago I found out just how important follow-up calls can be. I was following up with a phone call to a prospect I had met only once. He surprised me by saying he had been expecting my call and he would like me to come by his office.

When I arrived, he promptly outlined the needs he wanted me to address and then asked when I could start. It was an unusually quick sale. After agreeing on the details, we settled into a more informal discussion.

He related to me how a couple of weeks before my follow-up phone call he had been approached by another salesperson who pointed out a very specific need and then followed up with an elaborate proposal.

In discussing the proposal, he told the other salesperson that he already had a trusted consultant and that if anyone should do this project for him it would be his existing consultant. He went on, "Then after deciding it was something we really ought to do, I decided to wait for your call. I knew you would be giving me another call before too long."

This client reinforced the need in professional selling for keeping your name in front of valid prospects. I work hard at this in a number of ways including regular phone calls. When I need something extra to force me to get on the phone and make calls, I always think back to this memorable sale. How many more prospects might be waiting for my call? I wouldn't want to disappoint them.

– Submitted by Robert Lloyd Russell

The first impression

Whether on the phone, through email or in person, salespeople can make a positive first impression in various ways. At the same time, during the first meeting with prospects they can pick up on signals that indicate how the sales process is going. Jim Cathcart, founder and CEO of Cathcart Institute, shows how to manage first impressions to your advantage.

Be aware. Cathcart tells salespeople to be more aware of what's going on. Notice the prospect's feelings and emotions, and see if they shift during the meeting.

Be able to step back. Cultivate the capacity to think objectively while participating subjectively. Be in the sales dialogue and yet step back to see what's really going on. Make a mental checklist. Pick up on prospects' body language, tone of voice and other signals and interpret what they are saying. This enables you to ask the right questions and anticipate objections.

Turn the mirror around. Ask yourself: "How do I look? How is my customer seeing me? How am I being characterized? Do I give the impression I want?"

Manage intent. If you manage intent the content will take care of itself. Don't try to impress a new prospect. Know what you want to say and say it sincerely.

Jim Cathcart
Cathcart Institute

Sale #45

Follow Universal Teachings

BUSINESS BY THE GOLDEN RULE

Some years ago, when the nation of Libya was still a kingdom, I received a call from the Libyan Embassy in Washington DC to discuss having a flagpole installed at the chancery on Massachusetts Avenue. On arriving, I was escorted to my prospect's office – the office of the Ambassador. The Ambassador was a tall, distinguished-looking gentleman.

I listened attentively to his wants and needs and then presented to him what I proposed and how much it would cost.

He responded, "Your proposal is fine and agreeable, but what is my reduction?"

Reduction in this situation meant discount. My answer was, "I have given a fair price for both of us."

The Ambassador liked my proposal and product but still wanted a reduction. At that point, I was tempted to reduce the price because I desperately needed the order and job. However, I had offered an almost bare-bones quote to begin with.

Suddenly I had a thought and said, "Your Excellency, you are a follower of the teachings of Mohammed, the Prophet of Allah, and I of Jesus Christ, both of whom taught us to be fair in all of our dealings with all people and to do unto others as we would wish them to do unto us."

With that, he stood, extended his hand and said, "We do business." – *Submitted by Claude L. Haynes, Jr.*

Sale #46

Better Brainstorming

ONE NEW IDEA MADE MY BIG SALE

I'm a salesperson for a printing company. I started out as a typesetter. Mostly we do small jobs – business cards, letterheads, envelopes, advertising flyers and brochures. It's hard to get new customers, so it's worth giving the very best service to keep them.

My most memorable sale began a year ago when an insurance agent came to me for new business cards.

The insurance agent didn't like anything about the cards his company provided him at no charge. He was willing to pay me to design a better card to hand out to his prospects and clients.

I told him that his card should be one that no one would ever want to throw away or bury in a drawer. My experience as a typesetter has helped me understand type styles, graphics, printing methods

Goal getting

High achievements come from high aspirations, so follow this five-step plan from The Goals Institute president James R. Ball.

What do you want? Before you can set a goal, you need to know what you want. Assess your current position and how you got there and what changes you can make to take your performance to the next level.

Make a new plan. Ask yourself what's possible, what obstacles keep you from what's possible, and then what needs to be done to remove the obstacles.

Act now. Take your overall plan and break it down into a weekly plan. Have a daily plan or "thunderbolt list" of daily action items to carry you toward your goals.

Check your progress. Good plans get results. How do your results compare with your original expectations? The chances of developing the perfect plan out of the gate are about zero.

You'll need to adjust and refine it as you go along.

Make a habit of it. When you hit on something that works, do it until it's second nature. The true salespeople I know don't sit across from a customer and look for sales cues and think about when to go for the close. Their instincts tell them because they're on automatic pilot.

James R. Ball
The Goals Institute

and paper types and treatment, and I did my best to do a good job.

The insurance agent was very pleased with my design. The next week he brought two of his fellow agents, and I made identical cards for them, only changing the names.

Two weeks later the insurance company's regional manager wanted to see me. He asked if I would give a small discount if he ordered new cards for all his agents (257!) in a five-state region, using the card I had designed.

As a result of the creative assistance I gave to that first agent, we now do almost 2,000 orders of these cards each year – for new agents and for every time agents reorder, change location or position, or have new qualification titles added to their names.

– Submitted by Patricia Snead

Sale #47
Expect the Unexpected
ONE HUGGY BEAR

New England country auctions are a ritual. Each season we stage anywhere from six to nine estate auctions throughout our region of central Massachusetts. As an auctioneer I never really know what the next job will hold, both in gross sales and surprise items for sale. Each estate is unique; each auction, a challenge.

Last June I staged an estate auction in the tiny Massachusetts town of Royalston (population approximately 1,000). This particular estate included generations of antique furniture, furnishings and collectibles. We pitched two big striped tents – one green, the other one red – at a site that was in a hollow along the banks of the cold waters of the Lawrence Brook.

In working very closely with a woman who was executor of her mother's estate, I tried to be exacting every step of the way. All items were lotted and tagged. My anticipated bid-grabbers included primitive pieces of decorated stoneware. My hunch proved true when one old butter churn fetched $1,000 on the auction block. An 18th century lady's rocker moved to the tune of $1,800 – again no surprise. Next came the fun part.

Teddy bear, c. 1908, had won the hearts of the buyers and proved to be one of my most memorable sales as an estate auctioneer.

An unassuming teddy bear – full size, all brown and fluffy – received an opening bid of $100. I was delighted to see that somebody recognized value because this is what I had appraised the bear for before the auction.

Within seconds the bids began to escalate. Passing a bid of $500 alerted me that something special was going on. The $1,000 bid confirmed my belief. I didn't bat an eyelash as the bidding continued and reached $2,000. When the bidding got hot and heavy between the high bidder and the under bidder, one of them walked up to ask me a question. He asked if he could withdraw money from his savings account to cover the bid. I assured him that it would be fine. Then the other bidder shouted from the audience, "I wish I were included in the conversation." I immediately relayed the bidder's request to the audience and regained their attention, confidence and bidding.

Finally, when the bidding reached $4,200, the first bidder dropped out. Teddy bear, c. 1908, had won the hearts of the buyers and proved to be one of my most memorable sales as an estate auctioneer. – *Submitted by Robert L. Potvin*

Sale #48

Unforgettable Final Offers

HE OFFERED HIS BEST PROPOSAL, THEN HIS BLOOD

On my second visit to Egypt, my buyers put my selling skills to the acid test as I tried to close a $600,000 sale of electronic surveillance equipment. At the meeting site I learned that private negotiations would be held with each competing salesperson; then one would win the contract. When it was my turn, I sat down across from five buyer representatives from various fields of expertise, each of whom fired questions at me faster than I could answer. The "negotiations" quickly became an endurance contest. On the second grueling day of discussion, a buyer representative told me a competitor had offered "better performance, lower price, early delivery, software upgrades and a

---

Negotiation know-how

Achieve your ideal negotiating outcomes more often with Michael E. Sloopka's strategies to help you give maximum value to buyers at minimum cost to you.

Don't make concessions too soon. Start negotiating after you identify the opportunity for you and your company and your customer's buying behavior and greatest needs.

Follow negotiating protocol. For predictable results, don't just fly by the seat of your pants. Follow a disciplined process in order to achieve the desired results.

Negotiate in stages, in order. Establish opening positions (the buyer's first, then your own); seek additional information to determine how far apart your buyer's position is from yours; and reach for compromise once you know what's of value to your buyer.

Broaden your scope. You can negotiate dozens of other variables beyond price, terms and conditions. Be flexible.

Know what concessions you can make and what they cost. Remember that a concession's cost to you doesn't determine its value to the customer.

Adopt the right tactics and techniques. Predict your buyer's moves and how you'll respond. When a buyer says you have to do better, don't make a concession until you ask, "Exactly how much better do I have to do and in what area?"

Michael E. Sloopka
Selling Solutions Inc.

two-year warranty" and then asked for my "best and final offer." I retrieved a small penknife from my briefcase, passed it to the head negotiator, rolled up my sleeve, presented my arm and said, "Take the blood. It's all I have left to offer." He asked me to wait outside, then summoned me again after 15 minutes. All five negotiators stood at the table when I reentered. "Sign this," the head negotiator ordered. Fearing the papers he'd pushed in front of me were my death warrant, I hesitated, then glanced down to see the word CONTRACT at the top of the page. – *Submitted by Douglas Bonnot*

Sale #49
The Power of Concentration
WHERE THE WILD SALES ARE

During school vacations, I always take time off for a day in the city with my daughter. For several days prior to one such excursion, I'd been trying to get a prospect's feedback on a proposal. The decision deadline was drawing near, yet I was still unable to reach my contact. I told myself that my one day off wouldn't make a difference and asked my assistant to try to reach the prospect while I was out. On my day off, my daughter and I visited the zoo, where we enjoyed the beautiful weather and the animals. On the way to a sea lion feeding, my beeper went off. Eager for news about my elusive prospect, I dragged my daughter to a pay phone to call my office, only to find that the buyer had chosen another vendor with a lower price. To save the sale, I got permission to reduce our price. After instructing my daughter not to move out of my sight, I tried to rehearse my presentation, get my wits about me and concentrate on a phone call to my prospect. Surrounded by mothers and tired, whining children, I made my presentation – never disclosing my whereabouts. The next day, I found out that I got the sale. On my desk I keep a souvenir pencil from the zoo – a reminder of the power of concentration.

– Submitted by Patricia Bertell

Presentation preparations

Confidence boosts performance, so practice these pointers from professional speaker Dr. Donald E. Wetmore to soothe your nerves before presentations, negotiations and other stressful situations.

Prepare yourself. This is numero uno on the confidence-building scale. Prepare until you feel comfortable doing your presentation without notes. Practice in front of a mirror and in front of other people.

Connect with your audience. I try to get to the presentation site in advance and meet with the audience. Then when I start talking, I know I have some friends in the audience. Audiences are often very kind and sympathetic because they're glad they aren't the ones giving the presentation.

Envision victory. Visualize a positive outcome. To help dissolve your fear and its physical manifestations, picture your audience giving you a standing ovation or coming up to you afterward to say, "Wow, that was really dynamite. You really answered my questions and addressed the things that were important."

Tell yourself, "So what?" Can't shake the fear you'll blow it? So what? I used to share something called the "what if?" philosophy with the students in my business law class. When you think about whether your presentation might go badly, tell yourself, "So what?" It's not the end of the world. It's a learning experience.

Dr. Donald E. Wetmore
The Productivity Institute

Sale #50

Honesty Is the Best Policy

CREDIBILITY IS YOUR MOST VALUABLE ASSET

"Is your hydraulic hose-cutting machine OSHA approved?" asked the owner of a farm equipment dealership in central Wisconsin. It was an offhand question, thrown into the middle of my sales presentation along with many other questions and objections.

As a salesman for a wholesale distributor of hydraulic hose, fittings and crimping machines, I had been trying to sell this particular dealer for almost a year. Although he always listened to my presentations, so far he had not made a single purchase.

When we offered a special low price on the hose-cutting machine, I knew he'd be interested. His question about OSHA was not new to me nor did it require a detailed explanation. If not handled correctly, however, it could make the questioner, my prospect, look stupid.

The easy way was to just say, "Yes, it's OSHA approved," and go on with the presentation. Few people know that OSHA does not "approve" any product, so many salespeople just say yes and let it go at that.

Saying, "Yes, it's OSHA approved," never did sit well with me, so here's what I told this dealer and anyone who asked that question: "As you probably know, OSHA does not approve any products. However, the agency does provide safety guidelines for certain types of equipment. This cut-off machine meets or exceeds all OSHA safety guidelines."

The dealer nodded and I went on with my presentation. When I finished he bought the cut-off machine and actually went on to become a good customer. At the time, I had no idea how important the OSHA question had been in his decision to purchase.

About a year later, during a discussion of sales techniques, this same dealer asked me if I knew why he'd bought that hose cut-off machine from me and not from the other half-dozen or so salespeople who offered similar products.

"You were the only salesperson who told me the truth when I asked if it was OSHA approved," he said.

It's been many years since that sale but it taught me a valuable lesson – as a salesman, credibility is my most valuable asset. That's why I consider this my most memorable sale. – *Submitted by Paul Ferris*

Sale #51

Customers Are Number One

I LITERALLY PAINTED THE PROSPECT INTO THE SALE

One day my partner and I called on a liquor store that appeared to need one of our new outdoor, internally lighted signs. When I explained to the owner why we had stopped in, he began screaming about how he didn't need any "$$@#@! sign!"

"I personally know everybody in this town!" he yelled. "No %$**! sign is gonna bring in any new business!!"

Since I got the feeling he was not really a bad guy, I yelled back, "I've got a miniature model of the sign in my car. I'll show it to you – then you tell me if you don't think it'll bring in new business!"

He said, "Oh yeah! Well, go get the $%#* thing!" My partner mentioned the possibility that this might be a waste of our time, but I suggested we give it a shot.

I quickly found that he did know everyone in town. Every few minutes during our presentation, customers interrupted with news of grandchildren and political gossip. After about an hour of this, I decided to make one last ditch effort. My partner drew a layout for the proposed sign to match a mural that covered the outside wall of the store depicting King Kong towering over the New York skyline and pouring a big bottle of champagne with the face of the store owner inside one of the bubbles. I suggested that my partner sketch the mural on the proposed sign. I would show it to the owner, ask for the order and take cover.

"John," he said, "once you showed me my face up in the air in lights, that was enough. Paint my picture on the sign, and I'd buy it at any price!"

Just then a man from the city utilities came in to speak with the owner. After a moment together, the owner chased the utility man from the store screaming, "...and don't come back!" The owner turned to me and said, "Can you believe these people? Expect me to pay them $500 this month! They think I got $500 sitting around to give to any bozo who walks in and asks for it!"

I felt a little discouraged. In about one minute I was going to ask him for $650 as a down payment on a sign he felt he didn't even need. Nevertheless, I showed him the sign and the figures and prepared to grab my briefcase and run. He said softly, "I'll take it." There was total silence as I wrote up the paperwork. As we were about to leave I asked what had made him buy the sign.

"John," he said, "once you showed me my face up in the air in lights, that was enough. Paint my picture on the sign, and I'd buy it at any price!" – *Submitted by John R. Landrine*

Bait your hook

According to John R. Graham, president and CEO of Graham Communications, salespeople don't always have time to go out looking for customers. When you're too busy to go out fishing for customers, bait your hook so they come to you.

Become an invaluable resource. Salespeople and the company they represent must be an invaluable resource. They must show their knowledge and how it can solve their customers' problems. In addition, their problem-solving abilities must extend to unrelated products. This peripheral knowledge shows your customers that you really know your stuff and can handle any problem they might have. Get prospects to say, "I want to do business with you!"

Keep up with technology. If you have a Web site, align the information with what's in the customers' heads. Use a laptop to keep track of appointments, follow-ups and important dates. Use technology to manage the sales process.

Stick with your customers. Be on the radar screen all the time. When prospecting, send letters explaining what you will do over the long haul. Remain in constant contact. Establish a pattern and stick with it. Prospects will see that if you stick with them before a sale, they can expect it after a sale.

John R. Graham
Graham Communications

Sale #52

Double the Sales

HOW TO HANDLE TWO CUSTOMERS AT ONCE

Early in my sales career I learned how to handle a pair of potential buyers. The sale eluded me on this occasion; however, the wisdom gained helped in numerous situations after that.

The setting was a sales seminar. After the seminar my partner and I worked hard to close sales. This particular time I was discussing the benefits of our product with two individuals. It became apparent that one of them was much more open and positive to the offering. Instead of working and closing the positive prospect, I focused on the less enthusiastic buyer.

In theory I wanted to bring both along at the same pace. This didn't work. The positive prospect became more negative and both ended the day without enjoying what our service can provide.

The lesson learned was this – when dealing with a group of two, always close the positive prospect first and then go for the other sale.

Some time later the experience paid off. The same situation occurred. This time I was ready. The positive prospect asked the questions while the other fellow stood and watched. The objections came up and were handled. The closing questions were answered. The order from the positive prospect was finally secured. The less positive buyer had one question: "Whom do I make the check out to?" I knew the answer! – *Submitted by Kurt S. Pearson*

Sale #53

The Oooh-Aaah Close

OOOH-AAAH – I REMEMBERED ZIG ZIGLAR'S CLOSE

I was having trouble closing a sale to a couple who were looking for their dream home...until I remembered Zig Ziglar's oooh-aaah close. When I said that there was one last model to show them, situated on an exceptionally spacious site and ready for immediate occupancy, the husband interrupted, saying, "I bet I know which one you're talking about. Don't even bother to show it to us. If it's the one I think it is, it is so unattractive from the street, we needn't go inside."

I further described the home and the husband said, "Yes, that's it. We're not interested in that home." Then Zig took over.

"OK," I said, "I understand, but this is our oooh-aaah model. I guarantee that when you step through the front door you both will immediately start ooohing and aaahing nonstop."

They looked at each other and said, "We've seen everything else, we might as well take a peek before we leave."

As we walked through the foyer, their eyes lit up and they both began to compliment the design and use of space. After they took a preliminary look at most of the home I asked, "It's easy to see why we call it the oooh-aaah model, isn't it?" They both agreed.

We walked back outside and looked at the front of the home again and started trading ideas on small changes that would alter the appearance to make it a little more to their liking. We completed a sales agreement and they promptly moved in.

Continuing sales training and the proper use of it created a win-win situation and a most memorable sale. – *Submitted by Tom Alligood*

Sale #54

A Tie to the Rescue

DRESSED FOR SUCCESS

Everyone knows you must dress for success. My wife enjoys sewing and is talented, but there are times when I must question her taste. She made me a necktie with green and orange stripes, and I wore it to spare her feelings. It didn't look too good, but in my business as a representative for a medical supply company I often find myself in awkward situations, and the tie was soon to help me out of one of them.

I had gone to make a service call and instead wound up with a big sale and a happy client for my willingness to help with his problems.

Customers of all kinds keep me on my toes, but none so much as those at a certain veterinary clinic. On this morning Dr. Williams had telephoned to say he was upset. His office was having trouble installing an anesthesia vaporizer, so I drove over to see what I could do. Upon arriving I saw only empty chairs and old magazines in the waiting room, but heard an awful commotion coming from behind the closed door to the examining rooms.

When I walked back to investigate, I discovered Dr. Williams, his assistant, his receptionist and the owner of a large German shepherd all struggling with the animal, who had suddenly become excited. "This is what you get for not ordering our new model," I joked.

"What?" the harried veterinarian exclaimed. "Well, never mind that! Would you mind giving us a hand? Rex here is..." He cut himself short as the dog growled. It had been hit by a car and its leg was injured. I helped soothe the poor animal, and we gently muzzled it with my tie, which, believe it or not, was the only thing handy. Dr. Williams gave Rex an intravenous shot and, once things had calmed down, began treating the wounds.

The vaporizer itself was fine, I later explained, and I took the time to mention its advantages over conventional means of anesthesia. The veterinarian then made a large but unexpected purchase and thanked me for my assistance.

I had gone to make a service call and instead wound up with a big sale and a happy client for my willingness to help with his problems. I never found out what happened to the tie.

– Submitted by Joel Kline

Sale #55
Upselling Techniques
REV UP YOUR PRODUCT

One day a local Mercedes dealer called to give me the phone number of a client who had a Rolls-Royce for sale. I spoke with the seller regarding the details of the car and we agreed on a price. I told him I would overnight the check to him and pick up the car the next day. I then asked him if he was going to replace the car. He told me that he was considering a Mercedes convertible. I phoned over to the referring dealer and left a message. When this guy didn't call me back after two additional calls, I called a friend at a different Mercedes dealership, negotiated a price and finalized a deal with the client on the car. I told the customer I would deliver the car to him, then I contracted with a local trucking company to take the car.

Since the customer had made such a large purchase decision so quickly and had previously owned a Rolls-Royce, I decided to bring a brand-new Bentley and a brand-new Jaguar XK8 to show him. I

arrived at the customer's house early to build rapport with the client. As the transport turned the bend with the three cars, the customer asked what the additional two cars were for, and I told him I was hoping to tempt him. He laughed – then things began to go downhill. The truck driver had lost the keys to the Bentley, and it was blocking the other two cars so I couldn't get any of them off the truck. Finally, I disconnected the linkage at the transmission, rolled the Bentley back into his garage and got the other cars off the truck. Since the Bentley was so heavy, we could not get it back on the truck without the keys. I knew that it was going to stay overnight at the client's house. I invited him to negotiate the price with me.

In the end, what nearly turned into a disaster turned into a sale of all three cars. As for the original Mercedes dealer, three days later he left a message on my machine apologizing for not getting back to me and asking me if I had the client's phone number. He also said he thought he might be able to sell the client a car.

– Submitted by Gary Whitaker

Sale #56

Keeping Nerves under Control

KEEP YOUR COOL

When I first moved to Chicago to run the Midwest sales office for APAC TeleServices, I went after some big accounts and eventually got a call back from a very large retailer who requested a proposal. Four months after I presented a proposal for almost $1 million in services, the prospect called and invited me to lunch. As dessert was being served, my client told me he didn't know whether to entrust me with his business or give it to a similarly priced and qualified competitor. He told me he was going to flip a coin to decide, and if I called the toss correctly, I could have the business. I felt the color drain from my face. My palms began to sweat as I realized my client was serious, but I tried to maintain a composed facade and called "heads" as he tossed the coin. Heads it was, fortunately, and I got the order.

After some time I asked my client why he had decided to base such an important decision on a coin toss. He confessed that he had already decided to work with my company before he flipped the coin, but because I had seemed so calm and cool up until then he wanted to see if he could make me squirm. When I didn't, he said, that proved to him that I wouldn't fall apart when a big challenge presented itself. Showing my prospect that I could handle pressure showed I could also handle their business.

— Submitted by Hayley Weinper

Sale #57
Follow-Up Is International
PROMPT FOLLOW-UP BUILDS TRUST

After returning from a trade show in Tokyo, I spent a frustrating first day back at the office catching up on phone messages and stacks of correspondence. I stoically plowed through the mess, then forced myself to study the notes I'd taken and business cards I'd collected from the many people I'd met on my trip.

> I knew that many Japanese businesspeople insist on building trust with foreign manufacturers before placing orders with them.

Having done my homework before leaving for Japan, I knew that many Japanese businesspeople insist on building trust with foreign manufacturers before placing orders with them. My research indicated that prompt attention to trade show inquiries would help me earn that trust. With this knowledge in mind and despite a tremendous case of jet lag, I began faxing thank-yous to the Japanese visitors to our Tokyo exhibit.

About two weeks later I received a call from a Japanese prospect from Okinawa. "This is Akio Yamashita of Wako Boeki Incorporated," said the voice at the other end. "Mr. Maetoku, our company president, and I would like to come to Des Moines to visit your plant."

"I would be happy to have you," I replied, more than a little astonished. "When would you like to come?"

Two weeks later I met the two gentlemen at the airport where we greeted each other warmly. Having exchanged the customary pleasantries, I blurted out, "I'm flattered that you decided to fly all the way out here to see me, but can you tell me what prompted you to do this?"

"It's really quite simple," said Mr. Maetoku. "Of all the people at the two dozen American exhibits we visited at the Tokyo trade show, you are the only one who bothered to send us any kind of acknowledgment, though we specifically requested information from several companies. Furthermore, you responded promptly."

Since that visit, we have shipped thousands of dollars' worth of goods to that customer and have an ongoing productive relationship. Apparently, prompt follow-up speaks a universal language of competence and reliability. – *Submitted by Max Isaacson*

Creative follow-up

Successful follow-up requires persistence, punctuality and sometimes a good dose of humor, according to Anne M. Bachrach, president of AM Enterprises. She recommends the following ideas to help that prospect become a customer.

Don't procrastinate. Have a day planner. Ask your prospect when it would be good to call, and mark the day and time on your calendar. If no exact time is established, then call that day and make a specific appointment.

No matter what, call when you arranged to call. "People are amazed I call back on the day when I was supposed to," says Bachrach. She adds this puts the ball in the prospect's court, which is positive for the salesperson.

Just the fax. If follow-up calls are never returned, a humorous fax might do the trick. Bachrach suggests sending a fax asking what the "magic number" of phone calls is before the prospect calls back. She also suggests

sending a playful fax to the prospect offering various options for reasons why phone calls are not returned: "I'm not interested," "I left all the information in the car," "The dog ate the material you sent," and "Call me on ___." The prospect can then check an option and fax it back. Bachrach says a "fun fax" does get through. "Gatekeepers like the fax and pass it on."

Anne M. Bachrach
AM Enterprises

Sale #58
Out of This World
THE "CAPTAIN KIRK" CLOSE

A couple about to tie the marriage knot requested my DJ service for their wedding reception music. Then they seemed to vanish into thin air. We sent them the appropriate paperwork. When they didn't return it on time, we tried calling repeatedly but always got an answering machine. Although I left messages they never called back.

> By using humor to defuse a stressful situation, I took the pressure off my prospects and got a sale that might otherwise have been lost in space!

In a last-ditch effort to connect with the couple and save the sale, I left one final message. The groom-to-be had recorded their answering machine greeting in his best "Scotty" voice, desperately explaining to the caller that the ship's power was going down and he was giving Captain Kirk all he could, etc., then promising to call back later. Hoping that a little humor would help me get a call back, I assumed the role of Captain James T. Kirk and left the following message: "Captain's log, stardate 9057.2. Have been unable to locate the missing couple and our hails are going unanswered. I fear they may have been captured by Klingons. I will attempt this final hail in hopes they can still be helped..."

The very next day they came to our office and signed their contract. By using humor to defuse a stressful situation, I took the pressure off my prospects and got a sale that might otherwise have been lost in space! – *Submitted by Pat Bruno*

Sale #59
Using a Low-Key Approach
PARKING LOT SALES

Selling pressure relief valves for an oil field service company keeps me in close contact with buyers from the oil and gas, petrochemical, pulp and paper, and refinery industries, but on one cold call I decided to keep my distance. Once while making calls out of town I came to a manufacturing facility I didn't recognize. In the yard I noticed some new pressure vessels. I knew they would need valves, and I knew I could supply them.

Some prospects require an aggressive approach, but in this case, low pressure brought me and my company high profits.

Instead of barging into the office to ask for an appointment, I chose to show my prospect how much I respected his time.

While stopped in the parking lot, I called the facility from my cellular phone. When I told the receptionist who and where I was, she seemed to respect my consideration and gave me the buyer's name. When I reached him, I said, "Mr. Holt, my name is Jeff Skibin and I represent Black Gold Valve. I do not know if you have a need to buy what I have to sell, but could I ask you a few questions to explore the possibilities?"

My polite, direct and honest approach worked, and he agreed to see me. I listened carefully to his needs, then left with a $40,000 sale. When I asked if he would have seen me if I had just walked into his office, he said, "Absolutely not."

Some prospects require an aggressive approach, but in this case low pressure brought me and my company high profits.

– Submitted by Jeffrey Skibin

Sale #60
Asking for Referrals
WHEN PROSPECTING, ALWAYS ASK FOR A REFERRAL

Early in my selling career, when I had been selling for about a month, I scheduled an appointment with a former co-worker to see how he was doing.

I showed up right on time but he wasn't there. I waited a few minutes for him to arrive and he still didn't show up. I was ready to leave when I noticed that an advertising agency had opened next door to him. I decided to walk in and convinced the owner of the company to listen to a presentation. We talked for about 15 minutes and it became apparent to me that his agency didn't qualify as a

Referrals of fortune

To put yourself in a position to attract more high-quality clients through referrals, make the most of these tips from author, speaker and trainer Bill Cates.

1. Earn the right to be "referable." Consistently provide great value and superior service.

2. Network with people who may never become clients. Chose those who naturally meet and know the type of people you're looking to meet.

3. Expand your results by targeting niche markets.

Birds of a feather flock together and referrals get easier and better when you work in one or two niches.

4. Make the referral process all about helping others, not yourself. Ask satisfied clients to help you reach others whom they care about.

5. Keep your referrals' source up to date with your progress – your success or lack of it. They need to know you followed through on their help.

6. Say thank you for referrals with a small gift. Your appreciative source will be willing to

offer more referrals.

7. Get your new clients to thank the source of the referrals. When your new clients thank their friend or colleague, the source becomes a hero and you become even more referable.

8. Expect to get referrals. Establish a referral mind-set so you see all the opportunities for referrals as they present themselves.

Bill Cates
The Referral Marketing Institute

potential client. I was ready to leave when a little voice in the back of my head said, "Ask for a referral!" I did exactly that.

He thought for a few seconds and suggested that I drop in on a production company two floors below.

I headed down and told the receptionist that the owner of the ad agency on the fourth floor suggested I speak to her boss. I waited a few minutes and got to sit down with the owner.

He not only ended up becoming an excellent client of mine, but became a friend as well. He continues to give me business even though I am no longer with my old firm, and we have even worked together on a few projects. Best of all, he refers business to me and I to him. It has become a true win-win relationship.

If I hadn't decided to make that first cold call, I would never have gotten that business. – *Submitted by Barry Katz*

CONTRIBUTING EXPERTS DIRECTORY

Spring Asher is a co-founder and principal with Chambers & Asher Speechworks, an internationally known firm specializing in speech and media training. She is also the co-author, with Wicke Chambers, of the book *Wooing and Winning Business: The Foolproof Formula for Making Persuasive Business Presentations* (John Wiley & Sons, 1998). For more information, write 3353 Peachtree Rd. NE, Ste. M-30, Atlanta, GA 30326; call 404/266-0888; fax 404/364-3490; email speechworks@ speechworks.net; or visit www.speechworks.net.

Anne M. Bachrach is a speaker and trainer and is president of AM Enterprises. She teaches the art of building high-trust relationships through "Values-Based Selling." For more information, write 5378 Renaissance Ave., San Diego, CA 92122-5632; call 858/554-0136; fax 858/554-0545; or email anne@bachrachvbs.com.

James R. Ball is the president and co-founder of The Goals Institute which helps corporations and individuals see their potential and then achieve it through the establishment, pursuit and realization of goals. He is also the author of the book *DNA Leadership Through Goal-Driven Management* (Goals Institute, 1997). For more information, write 1850 Centennial Park Dr., Ste. 450, Reston, VA 20191; call 703/264-2000; fax 703/264-2408; email info@goalsinstitute.com or visit www.goalpower.com.

Myers Barnes is a speaker, seminar leader and author and is president of Myers Barnes Associates Inc., a consulting and sales coaching firm specializing in management, human potential and sales achievement. He wrote the book *Closing Strong, the Super Sales Handbook* (MBA Publications, 1997) and the audio and video training tapes Follow-Up. For more information, write PO Box 50, Kitty Hawk, NC 27949; call 252/261-7611; fax 252/261-7615; or email sellmore@interpath.com.

Marjorie Brody is a speaker and executive coach seminar leader and is president of Brody Communications Ltd., which specializes in presentation and communications skills training. She is the author of 15 books, including *Professional Impressions...Etiquette for Everyone*. For more information, write PO Box 8868, Elkins Park, PA 19027; call 1-800-726-7936 or 215/886-1688; fax 215/886-1699; email mbrody@brodycomm.com; or visit www.brodycomm.com or www.marjoriebrody.com.

Eileen Brownell is a speaker, trainer, consultant and author and is president of Training Solutions. She provides keynote addresses, seminars and workshops on topics including customer service, conflict resolution, communication and team development. For more information, write 153 Picholine Way, Chico, CA 95928; call 1-888-324-6100 or 530/342-6300; fax 530/342-6200; or email Trainstars@aol.com.

Bill Cates is a speaker, trainer, author of the book *Unlimited Referrals* (Thunder Hill Press, 1996) and creator of the Unlimited Referrals System. He is also president of The Referral Marketing Institute. For more information, write 2915 Fenimore Rd., Silver Spring, MD 20902-2600; call 301/949-6789; fax 301/949-8564; email BillCates@ReferralCoach.com; or visit www.ReferralCoach.com.

Jim Cathcart, CSP, CPAE is founder and CEO of Cathcart Institute. He is a psychological researcher, business consultant, trainer and author of 12 books, including *Relationship Selling* (Perigee, 1990) and *The Acorn Principle* (St. Martins Press, 1998). For more information, write PO Box 9075, La Jolla, CA 92038; call 1-800-222-4883 or 858/456-3813; fax 858/456-7218; email info@cathcart.com; or visit www.cathcart.com.

Kevin Daley is president and CEO of Communispond Inc., an international personal communications skills training company. He is also the creator of the Socratic Selling Skills Program and author of *Socratic Selling: How to Ask the Questions That Get the Sale* (Irwin Professional Pub., 1996). For more information, write 300 Park Ave., 22nd floor, New York, NY 10022; call 1-800-529-5925 or 212/486-2300; fax 212/486-2680; or visit www.communispond.com.

Kevin Davis is president of Kevin Davis Selling Systems LLC, which provides sales and sales management training. Davis' consultative sales program is based on his book *Getting Into Your Customer's Head* (Times Books, 1996). For more information, write 4115 Blackhawk Plaza Circle, Ste. 100, Danville, CA 94506; call 1-888-545-SELL or 925/831-0922; fax 925/831-8677; email info@customershead.com; or visit www.customershead.com.

Jeffrey Gitomer is president of BuyGitomer Inc., which specializes in unique consultative sales training. He is the co-author, with Ron Zemke, of the book *Knock Your Socks Off Selling* (AMACOM, 1999). For more information write 705 Royal Ct., Ste. 100, Charlotte, NC 28202; call 704/333-1112; fax 704/333-1011; email salesman@gitomer.com; or visit www.gitomer.com.

John R. Graham is president and CEO of Graham Communications, a consulting firm specializing in the insurance industry, public relations and advertising, with special emphasis on "magnet marketing and sales." For more information, write 40 Oval Rd., Ste. 2, Quincy, MA 02170; call 617/328-0069; fax 617/471-1504; email info@grahamcomm.com; or visit www.grahamcomm.com.

Andrea J. Moses is the director of Powerbase Performance Group. In addition to providing customized seminars on skill development, she has taught competitive bidding to many sales professionals. She is also the author of several books including *Street Smart Selling* (Powerbase Performance Grp., 1990). For more information, write 2 Bloor St. W, Ste. 100, Toronto, ON M4W 3E2, Canada; call 416/481-0635; or fax 416/482-5626.

Barbara Pachter is a keynote speaker, business communications trainer, coach and author of several books, including *The Prentice Hall Complete Business Etiquette Handbook* (Prentice Hall Press, 1994). She is also the president of Pachter & Associates, which offers seminars in writing, etiquette, presentation skills and networking. For more information, write PO Box 3680, Cherry Hill, NJ 08034; call 856/751-6141; fax 856/751-6857; email contact@pachter.com; or visit www.pachter.com.

Omar Periu is a public speaker, trainer, sales executive and author of several publications, including *Investigative Selling*. He is president of Omar Periu International and conducts seminars nationally and internationally on sales and marketing, motivation and success, sales management and communications. For more information, write PO Box 812470, Boca Raton, FL 33481; call 561/362-5565; or fax 561/362-6309.

Keith Rosen is a sales and business coach and the creator of Innovative Selling, an audio sales training program designed to help salespeople maximize their potential. He is the president of Profit Builders, a sales and executive coaching and training organization offering customized sales, leadership and personal achievement seminars. For more information, call 1-888-262-2450 or 301/424-5714; fax 301/424-9669; email info@ProfitBuilders.com; or visit www.ProfitBuilders.com.

Michael E. Sloopka is practice director, speaker and seminar director with Selling Solutions Inc. He specializes in strategic customer management and negotiating. For more information, call 519/836-6105; email michael@sloopka.com; or visit www.sellingsolutionsinc.com.

Lynne Waymon is president of Waymon & Associates. She is a speaker, trainer and author of books and tapes focusing on strategic networking, including *Smart Networking* and *52 Ways to Re-connect, Follow Up & Stay in Touch* (Waymon & Associates, 1993). For more information, write 622 Ritchie Ave., Silver Spring, MD 20910; call 301/589-8633 or 1-800-352-2939; fax 301/589-8639; email Lwaymon@aol.com; or visit www.ContactsCount.com.

Dr. Donald E. Wetmore is a speaker, personal executive coach and president of The Productivity Institute, a consulting firm specializing in time management and personal productivity. For more information, write 60 Huntington St., PO Box 2126, Shelton, CT 06484; call 203/ 929-9902 or 1-800-969-3773; fax 203/929-8151; email ctsem@msn.com; or visit www.balancetime.com.

Thomas Wood-Young is president of Wood-Young Consulting, which specializes in sales training, recruiting, coaching, motivating and team building. He conducts seminars and sales training workshops, often focusing on Web site development and marketing. For more information, write 15968 Longmeadow, Colorado Springs, CO 80921; call 719/481-4040; email tom@WoodYoungConsulting.com; or visit www.salestrainingplus.com.

INDEX

A
adding value, 54-55
Alligood, Tom, 78
Asher, Spring, 2

B
Bachrach, Anne M., 84
Ball, James R., 67
Barnes, Myers, 43
Beasley, Debra, 39
Bertell, Patricia, 71-72
Bertin, Micah, 6-7
Blanton, Boyd, 52-53
Boggs, John, 57
Bonnot, Douglas, 70-71
Brody, Marjorie, 25
Brownell, Eileen, 7
Bruno, Pat, 85
business cards, 17-18, 19-20

C
Cates, Bill, 87
Cathcart, Jim, 65
Cecchi, Greg, 61
closing, 3-4, 23, 34-35, 77, 78, 85
cold calling, 32-33, 52-53, 86, 87-88
competition, 10
competitive bidding, 15-16, 35, 54-55, 61, 62-63, 66, 70-71, 71-72
composure, keeping one's, 82
contacts, 41

creativity, 3-4, 8-9, 22, 34-35, 40-41, 51, 74-75, 78, 85
credibility, 73-74
customers,
  and building loyalty, 64
  and serving, 20-21, 36-37, 42, 58-59, 59-60, 67-68, 79-80, 80-81
  lost, 26, 57
  rapport with, 12-13, 20-21, 50, 73-74, 76
  showing appreciation for, 45

D
Daley, Kevin, 37
Davidson, Carol, 40-41
Davis, Kevin, 60

E
Early, Rick, 59-60

F
Ferris, Paul, 73-74
first impressions, 65
follow-up, 64, 83-84
Forster, Mike, 45

G
Garrison, Paul, 15-16
gatekeepers, 6-7, 24-25, 55-56
Gitomer, Jeffrey, 11
goals, 61, 67
Golden Rule, 66

Goldstein, Alan, 32-33
Goldstein, Maxine, 36-37
Graham, John R., 76

H
Haber, George, 24-25, 42
Hawkin, Richard B., 51
Haynes, Claude L., Jr., 66
Hirni, Brad, 46-47
Holland, Sam, 10

I
integrity, 62-63
international business, 15-16, 70-71, 83-84
Isaacson, Max, 83-84

K
Katz, Barry, 87-88
Kline, Joel, 79-80
Kranig, Thomas, 4-5

L
Landrine, John R., 74-75
Lehrer, Sy, 30-31
letters, 24-25
listening, 28-29
Logan, Randal J., 23

M
Madan, Raj, 43-44
Mathison, Charles W., 38-39
Miles, Alfred B., 19-20

Miskel, Chet, 3-4
Moses, Andrea J., 15

N
negotiation, 15-16, 35, 54-55, 62-63, 66, 70-71
networking, 46-47
Neumann, D., 27-28
Norton, Michael, 50

O
objections, overcoming, 26, 35, 50, 52-53, 57
obstacles as opportunities, 11-12, 38-39
O'Dunn Wick, Donna, 8-9
Oglesby, John, 48
opportunities, being prepared for, 1-2, 11-12, 39, 79-80
orders, asking for, 3-4, 4-5

P
Pachter, Barbara, 47
Pearson, Kurt S., 77
Periu, Omar, 29
persistence, 17-18, 19-20, 26, 34-35, 38-39, 50, 54-55
personal touch, 12-13
Pool, Chris, 11-12
Pope, Lester M., 54-55
Potvin, Robert L., 68-69
presentations, 1-2, 8-9, 10, 27-28, 34-35, 39, 49, 61, 70-71, 71-72
product benefits, 22
prospecting, 12-13, 14, 17-18, 19-20, 30-31, 34-35, 39, 40-41, 42, 45, 48, 50, 59-60, 73-74, 74-75

Q

qualifying, 20-21, 43-44

R

rapport,
   with gatekeepers, 6-7, 24-25, 55-56
   with customers, 12-13, 20-21, 50,
      73-74, 76, 80-81
referrals, 87-88
Rosen, Keith, 33
Rozin, Randall S., 20-21
Russell, Robert Lloyd, 64

S

Siles, Richard, 55-56
Simmons, Christopher, 14
Skibin, Jeffrey, 86
Slavish, Jim, 35
Sloopka, Michael E., 70
Snead, Patricia, 67-68
Snow, Brett T., 26
surprises, 30-31, 68-69, 79-80, 82
suspense, 8-9

T

Todd, Lisabeth B., 28-29
Thorpe, Richard, 22

U

upselling, 80-81

V

Van Dorn, Stuart N., 1-2
visualization, 49
visuals, 2

W

Watters, Jeffrey A., 49
Waymon, Lynne, 41
Weinper, Hayley, 82
Westenberg, Bob, 12-13
Wetmore, Dr. Donald E., 72
Whitaker, Gary, 80-81
Wilf, Charles, 34-35
Wilkinson, Robert Z., 17-18
Wilson, Bob, 58-59
Wood-Young, Thomas, 53
Worden, Jim, 62-63